A welcome companion for mothers in the first year of their child's life, *Soul Food for Mums* gently leads us in ~~biblical reflections~~ ... urney of motherhood. Never guilt-induc ... daily devotions), it can be nibbled at or ... nent. One I wish I had had when my kids were ... Amy Boucher Pye, writer and columnist

I wish I'd had a book like *Soul Food for Mums* when my babies came along and turned everything upside down. When my boys were little I was tired, disorientated and seriously unwell – not at all like the women on the cover of *Parenting* magazine. What a welcome relief, therefore, to read a book that is honest and open about the challenges, as well as the joys, of motherhood. Lucinda and Anna help us to discover new ways of loving, living and learning from God at a time when it's easy to throw out daily devotionals with the nappy bags. *Soul Food for Mums* will connect you in new ways with God's heart and healing, as you experience his amazing love for your little one.
Sammy Greig, 24-7 Prayer

This down-to-earth book offers a lifeline of spiritual encouragement to mums in the wonderful, yet chaotic and exhausting, first year of motherhood.
Katharine Hill, Director of Family Policy, Care for the Family

This book makes a great gift for a new mum. It is designed to help her through the first years of baby's life and what can sometimes seem like a spiritual desert. It is full of common sense, short meditations and practical suggestions.
Mary Pytches, author and speaker

During the early weeks and months of finding myself with a new baby, I was alarmed at how wholly disorientating the whole experience felt. *Soul Food for Mums* is uniquely placed and so aptly devised; Lucinda and Anna insightfully tap into the whirlwind of anxieties, pressures and cocktail of emotions new mothers can experience, and reassuringly guide them back into the safety and clarity of God's truth and perspectives. Each devotional offers enough to challenge and provoke food for thought, but is also delightfully non-threatening and accessible to even the most sleep-deprived, time-poor and emotionally bewildered reader! This is a most excellent and valuable addition to the bedside table of any expectant or new mother who is still determined to keep God at the centre of her motherhood.

Sarah Wynter, Deputy Editor of Youthwork Magazine, *Associate Director of Onelife and mum to Bethany*

Lucinda van der Hart
& Anna France-Williams

Soul Food for Mums

INTER-VARSITY PRESS
Norton Street, Nottingham NG7 3HR, England
Email: ivp@ivpbooks.com
Website: www.ivpbooks.com

First published 2011

British Library Cataloguing in Publication Data
A catalogue record for this book is available from the British Library.

ISBN: 978–1–84474–521–0

Set in Dante 12/15pt
Typeset in Great Britain by CRB Associates, Potterhanworth, Lincolnshire
Printed and bound in Great Britain by Ashford Colour Press Ltd, Gosport, Hampshire

Inter-Varsity Press publishes Christian books that are true to the Bible and that communicate the gospel, develop discipleship and strengthen the church for its mission in the world.

Inter-Varsity Press is closely linked with the Universities and Colleges Christian Fellowship, a student movement connecting Christian Unions in universities and colleges throughout Great Britain, and a member movement of the International Fellowship of Evangelical Students. Website: www.uccf.org.uk

This book is dedicated to our children,
Eliana, Skye and Joseph Douglas,
and our own mums,
Annabel and Esther Vinai,
who have taught us so much about motherhood.

Contents

Foreword

Louie and Anna are both friends of mine. I first met Louie when she was a teenager and I was a helper on a Christian houseparty – unfortunately for her, she was also in the dormitory I was responsible for. Even back then her commitment to the Lord was evident and impressive. Anna came with her husband, Azariah, to work on the staff team of our church a few years ago. Her faithfulness to the Lord and loyalty to friends shone out from the first time I met her. Anna was one of the few people I asked for prayer when I was pregnant with my third child, Benjamin, and it seemed likely that we would lose him. I will always be thankful for those prayers and her discretion.

The women writing this book are the real deal, and knowing them both made me want to read what they have to say about a mother's relationship with God during the early days of a child's life. For me the arrival of my twin boys was a complete revelation. My husband and I felt as if we could enter into a new dimension of relationship with God, grasping theological truths we had spoken about or sung in a deeper, more visceral way. It took months before I could sing 'And when I think that God, His Son not sparing, Sent Him to die, I scarce can take it in . . . ' without choking. Holding our precious twin sons, the depth of God's love for the world just poured into our souls.

On the other hand, the haze of sleeplessness, physical exhaustion and lack of uninterrupted time were a serious challenge to my devotional routines. When I look back, beautiful memories of times with God while I fed the babies stand out amidst the chaos and tiredness. I have a particularly wonderful memory of the week in which my parents came to stay after the twins were born. My father got up every night to help me with the babies and, while I fed them, we prayed and prophesied over the boys into the small hours.

The early weeks and months of life are such a gift, and that is why I was absolutely thrilled to read *Soul Food for Mums*. We hear so much negative comment about the tiredness and difficulty in coping with babies, that it can be tempting to lose sight of the privilege of the stage in life into which God has brought us. This book will help mothers to hold on to the Lord, glimpse the wonder of life and keep growing as Christian disciples in the early days of motherhood – rooted in the practical challenges of daily life, but not opting out of the purposes of God for our lives.

I commend Louie and Anna as faithful followers of Christ and I commend their book with its sensitive and practical insight.

Amy Orr-Ewing, UK Director of RZIM (Ravi Zacharias International Ministries) Europe
Oxford 2011

Preface

Not long after starting out on writing this book with Anna, I discovered that I was pregnant for a second time. Eleven weeks ago today, my husband, Will, and I were blessed with a beautiful baby boy. We were elated, just as we had been elated following the birth of our daughter less than two years previously. Thank goodness we had no idea what the following two months were to hold. Little Joseph was soon back in hospital with bronchiolitis, which was followed by a serious and unusual MRSA infection. In total Joseph and I spent twenty-one nights in hospital together, and many more days.

There were times when Will and I thought we might lose him; days when I thought I might lose my faith. During those weeks I learned something new about the power of 'intercession' – prayer on behalf of others. When I was simply too disappointed by God to speak to him, I held on to the knowledge that our friends and family were doing battle with God on our behalf. Somehow that boosted my flaky faith. I knew from having my first child that engaging with God during the early months of your baby's life can be tough – but this was entirely unexpected.

As you read this book, it is my deepest hope that you will sense compassion from Anna and me, for you, the mother of a young baby. My children are the best thing that ever happened to me – but at times I hurt most because of them. We all need to know God's presence and compassionate love during this season. May this book bring that experience closer.

Introduction

I slumped down on my sofa with a sigh, took a sip of tepid tea, reached for my journal and began to write. I was reflecting on my first week of motherhood. It had been mostly about bodily fluids: poo, sick, milk and tears. And that was just me, Anna! My new daughter, Eliana, had also brought with her moments of laughter, pain, joy and an end to lie-ins. What's more, my 'quiet times' had become so quiet that I suspected even God couldn't hear them, and the methods of prayer I had previously enjoyed had been condensed into a frantic 'Help me, Lord!'

I wasn't alone. Eighty per cent of the mums we interviewed said that they found their spiritual life difficult when children came along. 'I can rarely concentrate in church,' they said, or 'I never have time to sit down and read my Bible.' This is why Louie and I have written this book. Just as our physical bodies have changed shape through childbirth, our devotional lives need to change shape too.

Our hope is that *Soul Food* will become a friend to you in this first year of your baby's life, bringing you encouragement, laughter and occasionally a loving challenge as you navigate the voyage of motherhood. It may take a bit of perseverance, but we can find ways of connecting with God not in spite of the chaos, but in the midst of it, learning about him from our parenting experiences and praying 'on the go' as we walk, change nappies, feed, rest and play.

Lucinda (whom I know as Louie) and I were both searching for a devotional book like this that would support us through the first year of motherhood. Louie, whose daughter, Skye, was then nine months old, was finishing writing her first book, *The Pregnancy Book*, and had asked me, at five months pregnant, to read a draft version. As we talked, we realized that we shared a desire to write something to encourage mums through the first year of their baby's life. What you are holding in your hand is the result of our collaboration, written during my daughter's first year (during her naps and in the evenings). It wouldn't be here without Louie's stalwart determination to write with an active toddler in tow and, before long, a second bump. This book is proof that our God is a miracle-worker!

God doesn't just work miracles. He also accompanies us on our journey of motherhood. Isaiah 40:11 says, ' . . . he gently leads those that have young.' This verse has been a reminder to me to be gentle with myself because God is gentle with me. As mums we can be prone to feelings of guilt, inadequacy and worry. Will we instead allow God to gently lead us? Will we take up the challenge of following his lead, no matter what this year has in store?

Whether you are a first-time mum, a mum of many, a mum in employment, a single, married or adoptive mum, we hope that *Soul Food* will help to sustain and nourish you. Not everyone comes to motherhood with a sense of delight – many of our stories relate a history mixed with broken-ness and pain – but, with God's leading, this year can be one of opportunity, discovery and spiritual growth.

How to use this book

Our vision is that *Soul Food* will be a book you can throw into your changing bag, read on the bus or keep in the kitchen to read as you stir the pasta. We want you to be able to enjoy refreshing time with God this year and, through connecting with him, connect better with your baby and those you are close to.

The bite-sized devotions are designed to suit whatever spiritual appetite you may have, from 'peckish' to 'starving'. Each one contains a menu of suggested ideas for action you could take in response to what you have read. Some weeks you may have enough time for all the activities, but other weeks you may manage only one. There may be months when you don't pick up the book at all: feel free then to jump on to the next month. Just dip in and out without feeling guilty.

Here's a guided tour:

- *Monthly themes:* Each month has a theme appropriate to what you may be going through at that stage of your baby's life.

- *Weekly reflection on Scripture:* Because we know that most mums don't have a lot of spare time, we have written weekly devotions rather than daily ones.

- *Act and pray:* The purpose of this weekly prayer idea is to get you praying and doing. Some ideas work better if you can find a bit of time to yourself (perhaps when your baby is sleeping, during your work lunch hour or when someone can babysit).

- *If you've got time:* This section gives you further prayer ideas and Scripture to look up, if and when you have a spare moment. The 'Your notes' section at the end of the book gives you space to jot down any thoughts, ideas or memories throughout the year.

- *Quote from a mum:* We have included stories and quotes from a variety of mums, so as to broaden out the perspectives offered from ours alone.

- *Related to this theme:* At the end of most of the devotions, we let you know of another devotion in the book that looks at a similar theme. If you feel inspired to read a little more one week, you can use this to direct you.

- *Profile of a mum:* Every three months we have included a relevant story from a mum to inspire you.

- The devotions are written alternately by Louie and Anna, as is indicated at the start of each one.

Cast your mind forward twelve months. Your copy of *Soul Food* may look pristine now, but by the end of the year we hope and pray that it will be dog-eared, covered in baby sick, spattered by pasta sauce and in the hands of a spiritually well-fed mum to a one-year-old.

Happy reading!

Anna and Louie

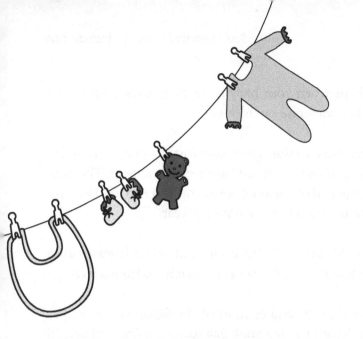

Month 1: Carried by God

Week 1: Our Creator God

By Louie

> Shout for joy to the LORD, all the earth.
>   Worship the LORD with gladness;
>   come before him with joyful songs.
> Know that the LORD is God.
>   It is he who made us, and we are his;
>   we are his people, the sheep of his pasture.
> (Psalm 100:1–3)

It is hard not to be in awe of the creative power of God afresh when you have recently given birth. Had I ever really previously understood what it meant that God is our Creator, as verse 3 above says? Having brought my daughter, Skye, home from hospital, I would look at her sleeping in her Moses basket, and find that thanks and praise tripped off my tongue as I marvelled at the amazing creative power God has invested in humankind.

At the same time I was a wreck. Physically drained from the birth experience, uncertain about how to breastfeed, and delirious with exhaustion and excitement, I spent the first few nights at home wondering how you get a newborn to sleep. Will and I soon found that Skye's car seat seemed to be her preferred sleeping location, and I immediately started worrying about whether we would ever manage to get her to sleep anywhere else. I had had almost no prior experience with babies and felt entirely out of my depth.

I also felt a deep sense of responsibility from the moment my daughter was placed in my arms, which took me by surprise. This tiny person was dependent on me for survival! And just as your newborn depends on you for existence, so you have been created to be dependent on God. We can have a special, intimate relationship with God, who is our Maker, our Parent, our Father. In Romans we read: ' . . . those who are led by the Spirit of God are the sons [or daughters] of God' (Romans 8:14).

You and I are built for that parent–child relationship with God. Without him, we lack the love and sustenance we need to survive. Katy, mum to Aurora, said, 'My baby was a constant reminder that God loves us intensely and devotedly, and provides for our every need . . . like a mother, in whose presence we can rest safely, and who, if we wake afraid or hungry, will comfort and feed us.'

Lean on God as you face the unknown of becoming a mum for the first time, or of changing your family dynamic by adding a new member. If you feel that you do not yet know God as your loving Father, ask him today to forgive you for your sins and accept you as his child, just as you lovingly accept the child you have brought into the world.

This week, invite God to be with you in the confusion brought on by tiredness, the physical pain as you recover from birth, and the moments of joy with your newborn. Allow him to carry and nurture you through this first month, as you do the same for your child.

 Act and pray

To pray an 'arrow' prayer is to shoot a speedy, miniature message up to heaven – where it is as well received by God as if we had been on our knees for hours. This week, shoot arrow prayers to him, thanking him for your new baby, and asking him for help and healing.

If you've got time

1. Look up Romans 8:14–17 in your Bible. In verse 15, we read that, because we are God's children, we can cry out to him, addressing him as 'Abba, Father'. The word Abba has no direct translation from the language Jesus spoke (Aramaic) – it was a unique expression of the close relationship between parent and child. Perhaps the closest English word is 'Daddy'. Enjoy communicating simply and intimately with God, your Daddy.

2. Write a letter to your baby, telling him or her how you felt on meeting for the first time. What was it like to show them their first earthly home and introduce them to their family? Store your letter somewhere safe – it will be a beautiful and precious gift for them in years to come.

3. When Jesus was born in Bethlehem, his parents Mary and Joseph received several important visitors – wise men and shepherds.[1] Pray for strength to enjoy the visitors who come to see you and your baby in the next few weeks, and wisdom to draw the necessary boundaries so that you can also have time as a family.

'The first few weeks can be a very barren time spiritually – don't have too high expectations of yourself, and allow God to carry you through. The tiredness and newness of becoming a mum doesn't last for ever. During this time, rely on God and hold the promises he has given to you close to your heart.'

Sam, mum to Charlie, three, Jessica, eighteen months, and twenty weeks pregnant

Related to this theme:
Month 7, Week 2: A childlike faith

Month 1: Carried by God

Week 2: The God who watches over us

By Anna

There are few things in this world as beautiful as watching a contented baby sleep. During the first night in hospital after my daughter, Eliana, was born, I could not peel my eyes from her exquisite face as she slept in my arms. When I finally placed her in the crib, I experienced an overwhelming feeling of love and a powerful desire to protect her in her vulnerability. I did not want to sleep in case something happened to her. Her 7lb frame was so fragile and delicate. What if she never woke up? As I lay there I was aware of every sigh and shuffle.

Weeks later, when she slept through the night for the first time, I woke up with a jolt at 8 am, realizing she hadn't woken up for a feed. I rushed over to her crib and relaxed as I saw the steady rise and fall of the blanket covering her tiny beating heart. I had always thought that mothers who did that were neurotic!

Having a baby gave me a new understanding of Jesus as a vulnerable newborn baby. He was born in insanitary conditions at a time of political instability – his parents must have worried about his well-being, just as we worry about that of our children.

Our fears as parents can be totally irrational, but they are also very normal. They can be paralysing, or they can be an opportunity to trust God.

> He will not let your foot slip –
>   he who watches over you will not slumber;
> indeed, he who watches over Israel
>   will neither slumber nor sleep.
> (Psalm 121:3–4)

Psalm 121 was probably written for pilgrims who were on their way to a religious festival – pilgrims who had to trust God for the many uncertainties and dangers on their journey.[2] Unlike the many gods that people worshipped at the time, Yahweh was always alive and awake.[3] He is the God who watches over us as our 'Guardian' or protective presence.[4]

We can't stay awake all the time, but God can. We won't always be by our baby's side, but God will. We don't yet know how many breaths and heartbeats are numbered in our child's life, but God does. We don't know how our baby's body knows to keep doing the things that keep him or her alive, but God formed that body and breathed into it the life we now long to protect.

So when you close your eyes and rest, know that God is still gazing at that curled form, transfixed by the beauty of the life he has created. He is the greatest parent of all, the God who watches over us.

 Act and pray

As you put your baby to sleep this week, repeat a simple prayer like the following: 'Jesus, thank you for watching over my baby.' As you fall asleep (whatever the time of day!), thank God for watching over you.

If you've got time

1. As you dress your baby each morning, pray for God's protection over every area of his or her life. Here are some starting points:

   - Pray for physical protection over your baby's health
   - Pray for emotional protection over their heart as they grow up and begin to form relationships
   - Pray for spiritual protection against the lies of the world as they grow older

2. When we are fearful, we need God's peace. The Hebrew word for peace is 'shalom', which means a broad sense of well-being, encapsulating health, prosperity, security, friendship and salvation. Shalom comes from God's presence with his people and favour towards them.[5] When you feel fearful or vulnerable this week, ask God for his shalom.

3. Try praying the 'prayer for sleep' below, when you wake in the night to feed your baby.

A prayer for sleep

Lord, thank you for the gift of sleep: for its mystery, its dreams, its renewal.

I pray for sleep for my child: sleep that is undisturbed, except to take in the nourishment to grow, sleep that is peaceful and safe in you.

I pray for sleep for myself, sleep that is relaxed and restful because I can trust you with my fears, and with my baby. I praise you that, when my eyes close, yours are still open and watching over the crib beside me. 'I will lie down and sleep in peace, for you alone, O LORD, make me dwell in safety' (Psalm 4:8).

Thank you, Father, that all through the night, whatever it holds, you never leave our sides, and that ' . . . when I awake, I am still with you' (Psalm 139:18).

Amen.

Written by Ruth, mum to Isla, five, Carys, two and Keira, six months

 Related to this theme:
Month 5, Week 3: God with you through your child's suffering

Month 1: Carried by God

Week 3: Light in the darkness

By Louie

At three or four in the morning, as you struggle to feed, wind or settle your newborn, the physical darkness can seem a bleak and lonely place. During those night hours I would sometimes think about mums of young babies across the globe who must also be losing sleep, or those whose jobs required them to work nights. It reminded me that I wasn't alone.

Jesus says, 'I am the light of the world. Whoever follows me will never walk in darkness, but will have the light of life' (John 8:12).

The 'darkness' that we experience as a mum of a newborn may not only be the literal blackness of night, but also a heaviness of spirit. I used to feel so helpless as I listened to my baby cry – I was desperate to settle her but couldn't do so. This is where Jesus brings his gentle yet powerful light. Where we are walking in the shadows, he lifts our spirits enough for us to cope again. Where we cannot see a resolution to the problem before us, he throws a fresh perspective on our situation.

To have faith is to believe, even when we cannot physically see God. A season of facing the darkness of loneliness and despair (rather than the darkness of sin) can bring a new meaning to the very concept of faith. When we have nothing left to give and can no longer depend on our own abilities, our only option is to trust. It's in this place that we realize that, with God's power behind us, we can in fact do and see things far beyond our natural capacity. The psalmist expresses this beautifully:

You, O LORD, keep my lamp burning;
    my God turns my darkness into light.
With your help I can advance against a troop;
    with my God I can scale a wall.
(Psalm 18:28–29)

Act and pray

Light a candle and, as you watch its flickering flame, reflect on this promise from John's Gospel: 'The light shines in the darkness, and the darkness has not overcome it' (John 1:5, ESV).

A prayer inviting God to bring his light:

'Come, light of the world, and brighten up my corner of the universe. When I am awake at night in the darkness, give me a sense of your presence and light. Bring clarity where I cannot see what to do. Please lift my mood on the days when I feel low, and give me fresh hope in you. Amen.'

If you've got time

1. When your baby next cries and your first instinct is to panic, invite Jesus into the situation with you. You might simply pray, 'Lord, help me to discern what to do. Throw your light on this situation and give me your wisdom.' Reflect on these verses from Job:

> But where can wisdom be found?
>   Where does understanding dwell?
>
> The deep says, 'It is not in me';
>   the sea says, 'It is not with me.'
>
> God understands the way to it
>   and he alone knows where it dwells.
>   (Job 28:12, 14, 23)

2. Ask another Christian to pray with you about the challenges you currently face as a mother. We may think that the things about which we are concerned for our newborn will seem insignificant to other people. But if they are worries for you, don't dismiss them as ridiculous. Bring them to God in prayer: he cares about even the smallest of details.

3. Look up Romans 5:1–5. As you push your baby in his or her pram this week, worship God with short prayers of thanks, even if you are in the

midst of tough times. Allow nature's beauty to inspire your praise. Stormie Omartian writes: 'When we praise God in the midst of our sickness, pain, weakness, or misery, our act of worship opens up a channel through which His healing presence can penetrate our lives to heal us or sustain us as He sees fit. That is the hidden power of praising God.'[6]

'As a new mum, there were times when I did not know what to do . . . All I could do was ask God to help me. Once we were at a wedding, and Isaac was beside himself. It might have been obvious to an experienced mum, but I had no idea what to do. I prayed and sensed that Isaac was over-stimulated by the busyness of the day and needed some space. This calmed me and enabled me to take him away from the crowd. The important thing about this experience for me was the sense that God was as concerned with the details of what this baby needed as I was; a sense that we were in it together.'

Joy, mum to Isaac, ten, Caleb, eight, and Moses, one

Related to this theme:
Month 3, Week 2: Feeling alone

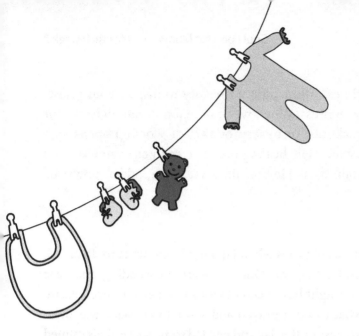

Month 1: Carried by God

Week 4: Nourishing your baby

By Anna

'Ow!' I exclaimed for the fifth time that day. 'Ow, that really hurts!' My greedy newborn was biting down on my nipple again as I attempted to feed her. In the first week of my daughter's life, I felt that all I was doing was feeding her. At one point during the night it was as relentless as every half hour! My breasts were red raw and extremely painful, yet she still kept feeding. 'How can someone so small require so much food?' I thought despairingly.

Despite the challenges, I loved seeing my daughter's satisfied face after a feed. Full of milk, she would sigh with contentment, close her eyes and stick out her bottom lip. I knew that, in order for her to be full, I needed to eat healthy, calorie-rich food myself. My friend had taken this very seriously and sent me the most delicious West Country fudge while I was still in hospital, as it was apparently good for breastfeeding. It tasted heavenly! Unfortunately, those who visited me also discovered this, so it didn't last very long.

In the weeks after giving birth our own health can sometimes suffer at the expense of our baby's. In the first month I remember finally getting round to making soup for lunch at 3 pm but then having to abandon it to comfort Eliana, and returning only when it had gone cold. Whether you choose to breastfeed or bottle-feed, it's hard to keep yourself physically, emotionally and spiritually nourished when you have a newborn to feed and care for.

But in the midst of this life change it is possible to allow God to nourish us with his goodness, just as we nourish our babies with milk. At a time of anxiety and fear, when on the run from King Saul, David wrote in Psalm 34:8: 'Taste and see that the LORD is good; blessed is the [wo]man who takes refuge in him.'

During those early months I could barely find my Bible, let alone read it, yet I was able to remember the Lord's goodness and to 'feed' on him, however haphazardly. 'Tasting' God sometimes meant a quick prayer of thanks for Eliana's health, or an acknowledgment of his presence in a situation where I felt anxious, such as the first time I took her out on my own. This 'tasting' was sometimes just enough to help me to remember the Lord's goodness. It is comforting to know that, as we allow ourselves to be nourished by God, he takes the same delight in seeing us satisfied as we do in looking at our milky-faced babies.

 **Act and pray**

This week, why not use each feed as an opportunity to pray? You could pray for a different friend, family member or need each time.

If you've got time

1. Buy your favourite food this week (or ask someone else to), and, as you eat it, savour the texture and flavour. Ask God to nourish you physically, emotionally and spiritually. Pray a prayer of commitment to your heavenly Father as you embark on this new season of motherhood.

2. If feeding your baby has been a challenging experience so far, ask God for wisdom. Give him your pain, your disappointment and your hopes for the future. If feeding your child has been a pleasure, use your mobile phone to take a photo of your child's face after they have enjoyed a feed. Look at the photo this week and use it to pray for your baby.

3. There are many passages in the Bible that use imagery from motherhood and feeding (Isaiah 49:15 and 1 Peter 2:2–3, for example). Read these passages and thank God for the way in which he nurtures and feeds you like a mother.

'When I had a baby, "quiet times" as I knew them went out of the window. I found that I had to use little pockets of time, like while feeding my baby, to pray. It was a great opportunity to talk with God and it kept me sane. My overwhelming feelings of love for my little bundle of joy gave me a new depth of understanding of God's love. I felt like I had a new appreciation of God's feminine, maternal side. As women are made in his image,

I guess it makes sense that he would have a feminine side, but in the past I always saw God as entirely masculine. I have got to know God as my heavenly Father, but only recently have I felt him mothering me too.'

Hazel, mum to Zephan, eight months

 Related to this theme:
Month 8, Week 1: Listening to God

Profile of a mum

Focus: Tiredness

When I was pregnant I remember hearing other mums talk about how hard the first few weeks were. I always brushed this aside and thought I would be fine. 'How bad can it be? I will pray through the hard times,' I thought to myself.

Caitlin was born after a thirty-nine-hour labour, and after a few days of no sleep and constant crying (from both of us), it hit me what all these mums had been talking about. All of a sudden I wanted to hug them and howl out, 'I feel your pain!'

The lack of sleep and crying took its toll on me, and I started to struggle to feel loving towards Caitlin. During my pregnancy daydreams I had always imagined feeding Caitlin at 3 am and singing gentle songs of love over her while rocking smoothly in my nursing chair. Instead, I was a grouch who huffed and puffed at the thought of yet another night feed.

Because of my unexpected behaviour I started to feel guilty and a failure, because I had not lived up to the wonder-mum ideal that I had dreamt about.

I found myself having to ignore the little whispers of lies such as 'You're really rubbish' or 'Poor Caitlin, having a mum like you', and actively focus on the good points from the day. I started to name these 'my little nuggets of joy'.

Such nuggets of joy came in different ways and gradually became more frequent. Sometimes they came in a special moment between Caitlin and me, or while watching my husband, Mark, with her.

I remember the day when she belched so loudly that we started to nickname her 'Barney' (from *The Simpsons*), or the day she fell asleep on her daddy with her mouth wide open. Those moments I will treasure and hold on to.

The natural love and patience which I had thought would be there towards Caitlin became more of a daily choice. This was not because I was depressed, a rubbish mum, or didn't love Caitlin, but because I was sleep-deprived and couldn't rely on my feelings, so I had to make a choice for each day.

Motherhood was (and is) such a shock to the system and affects all areas of life – emotional, physical, mental and spiritual. We are not in it alone, however. Sharing my worries with God and with close friends really made a difference. You soon discover that you are not the only one struggling to keep your cool in the night, and everyone else does not have the model child who sleeps, eats and burps on cue.

When I eventually started to get some sleep, everything became much clearer and I began to see the truth. I'm a good mum – not judged by how I do or how I react during tough times, but because I have a love for Caitlin which is continually growing.

Lydia, mum to Caitlin, four months

Month 2: A Season of Change

Week 1: Baby first

By Anna

> [Jesus] . . . got up from the meal, took off his outer clothing, and wrapped a towel around his waist. After that, he poured water into a basin and began to wash his disciples' feet, drying them with the towel that was wrapped around him.
> (John 13:4–5)

I was in a church service with Eliana, notebook out, pen poised and ready to receive the Word of God. The lady next to me turned towards me, held her nose and signalled at my whiffy baby. Uh-oh, time for a nappy change.

I was an expert at super-speedy nappy changing, so saw this as an opportunity for a personal challenge: get back in before the sermon ends.

Rushing to the changing room, I discovered that her super-size poo had squelched out of the side of her nappy on to her new Sunday dress. I cleaned her up and dressed her in her spare set of clothes in record time, eager to get back to the sermon. Just as I put on the new nappy, she began to wee again, spraying the changing table. Time for another nappy change.

Ten minutes later we were ready to go. Then Eliana decided to vomit down her fresh set of clothes. As I hurriedly wiped her and rushed back to my seat, I heard the minister's words: 'And now let's pray as we close . . . '

I don't often feel very holy when I'm changing Eliana's nappy for the sixth time in a day, or when I'm cleaning up vomit from the carpet. Listening to a sermon in church feels like much more of a holy act.

Sometimes we forget that Jesus was very used to the earthy things of life, having spent years as a carpenter before becoming a rabbi. His washing of the disciples' feet, which would have been grimy from the day's walking, was a powerful act of love. The disciples would have felt embarrassed by their master's humble act, which said as loudly as words, 'I am here to serve you in love.'

Richard Foster talks about 'praying the ordinary', which means that our work *becomes* acted-out prayer as we offer it lovingly to God.[1] Even mind-numbingly boring work is highly valued in the kingdom of God if done for his glory. Nappy changing can indeed be a sweet-smelling offering rising to the throne of the King!

Our baby's needs may have to come before our own in a practical sense at this time, but our unglamorous work is far from being a hindrance to our relationship with God. Discovering God at the heart of our ordinary, daily routines can transform us into passionate and purposeful Christian mums. Can you begin to see every activity of your day as a 'holy habitat of the eternal', a place in which God can be found and communed with?

Reflect on this challenge as you read this quote: 'Ordinary things have an extraordinary value in the eyes of God, especially when done as acts of love, love of God and love of the family. But their special value comes from the fact that God became man, lived a family life in Nazareth with Mary and Joseph, and thereby sanctified the ordinary and gave it meaning.'[2]

Act and pray

This week, change nappies, clean up and care for your baby as prayerful acts of love to God. Spend a few moments with God as you work. Be honest with him about how you're feeling and ask him to help you love your baby sacrificially.

If you've got time

1. Invite God into your daily household chores by praying these prayers used by Chinese Christian women:

   When washing clothes:
   I pray thee, Lord, to wash my heart, making me white as snow.

   When sweeping (or vacuuming) floors:
   I pray thee, Lord, to sweep away my heart's uncleanness, that my heart may always be pure.

When boiling water for tea:
I pray thee, Lord, to send down spiritual fire to burn away the coldness of my heart and that I may always be hot-hearted in serving thee.[3]

2. Many mums of newborns say that sleep deprivation is the toughest challenge of early motherhood. When you feel tired this week, try some breathing prayer. As you breathe in, ask God to fill you with his love. As you breathe out, breathe out your frustrations and concerns.

3. It can be easy to think of the mundane things we don't enjoy about motherhood. Write a list of the experiences that you regularly enjoy with your baby, and thank God for these gifts.

'I used to grind my teeth when I was doing chores, but now I try to say, "Christ, shine on me, Christ shine through me, I'm going for it." God can really speak to you, even when you are washing up. In the evening, I've started to make the washing-up time a period of silence. I let God's peace come, and the stillness settle within.'

Susie, mum to Jed, four, and Lily, fourteen months

Related to this theme:
Month 10, Week 1: Loving your child

Month 2: A Season of Change

Week 2: A new family member

By Louie

> Carry each other's burdens, and in this way you will fulfil the law of Christ.
> (Galatians 6:2)

On your baby's arrival in the world, a fundamental shift occurred in your family status. Once you were a couple, and now you are a family of three. Or, if you already have other children, you now have a very different future ahead of you as a larger family. If you are parenting alone, you and your child now form your own family unit. I wonder if you have had a chance yet to reflect on these changes?

Couples often say that having a baby unites them afresh as a couple. Indeed, 50% of the mums we talked to while researching this book said that their husband was their greatest support in their walk with God through the first year of motherhood. Catherine, mum to Sophia, three, and Joshua, fifteen months, said that, when she had her first child, 'I hadn't anticipated the joy of sharing our daughter's developments with my husband – watching her sit up for the first time together, or the excitement of telling him at the end of a day what she had been doing.'

At the same time, navigating the first few weeks with a young baby at home is a challenge to the very strongest of relationships. It's easy to compare what you are doing and giving with your husband's experience of a normal day – which is perhaps suddenly vastly different from your own – and to resent his freedom. Exhaustion can leave us snappy and bitter towards the person we love most in the world – just when we need each other more than ever before!

Step into your husband's shoes for a moment. What challenges is he facing as a dad? Is he struggling to deal with tiredness as he returns to work after paternity leave? Is he wondering how best to help you in your role as mum? Does he feel emotionally ousted as you move from investing your energies in him to spending yourself on your baby?

The verse above simply calls us to 'carry each other's burdens'. This may mean practically sharing the new load of jobs that come with a baby, but it also means communicating and connecting emotionally. Are you prepared to see your husband's perspective on life at present, and seek to bless him in that place?

 **Act and pray**

Talk to your husband and find a time that will be quiet so you can pray together. Share the things you would like prayer for, and how you would like God to work in your relationship at the moment. You might like to pray about:

- Your relationship in this particular season. Ask God to show you how to improve your communication, forgive each other where necessary and creatively find ways to do things differently.

- Your baby. Not long after Jesus was born, Mary and Joseph presented him to God together.[4] You could set aside a special time to pray together for your child, dedicating his or her future to God. If you haven't prayed for your baby together before, this can help draw you closer as a couple.

- Other people to support your marriage. Are there friends, perhaps from church, whom you can ask to pray specifically for your relationship at the moment? Ask God to help you discern whom to ask. If you are parenting alone, meet to pray and share accountably with a close friend or family member. What particular challenges do you currently face as a single mum? Turn to our Resources section on page 230 for information on support for lone parents.

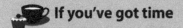 **If you've got time**

1. Contact an older couple from church, asking them to pray for your marriage over the next six months. Ask for their advice on keeping your marriage strong when you have a young baby to care for.

2. Come up with a small way in which you could bless your husband this week. Perhaps write him a card, thanking him for his love and support. If you are parenting alone, do this for a friend or parent who has been there for you since your baby was born.

3. Reflect on these words:

> Every experience of love gives us yet another glimpse of the meaning of love in God himself . . . Human love reflects divine love and, indeed, transmits it.[5]

'The thing I repeatedly found myself asking forgiveness for during the early months of parenthood was the way in which I had no energy and very little patience left to deal with my husband. At these times of anger and crisis, we would not attempt to reason things out – just stop and (sometimes very angrily) hold hands and say a prayer. Often this was only the Lord's Prayer. We noticed a massive improvement in our mutual harmony when we remembered to say daily prayers together . . . but, failing that, emergency prayers were our lifelines.'

Katy, mum to Aurora, ten months

 Related to this theme:
Month 2, Week 4: Patience in the storm

Month 2: A Season of Change

Week 3: Identity shift

By Anna

> And Mary said:
> 'My soul glorifies the Lord
>   and my spirit rejoices in God my Saviour,
> for he has been mindful
>   of the humble state of his servant.
> From now on all generations will call me blessed,
>   for the Mighty One has done great things for me.'
> (Luke 1:46–49)

I wonder what Mary, Jesus' mother, felt on hearing that she would be mother to the Messiah. One moment she was just 'Mary from down the road' and the next she was the 'bearer of the one who would save the world'. When it comes to a change in identity, this one was pretty radical!

I love the way Mary sings praise to God, expressing her awe and wonder at the cosmic significance of the news that she will give birth to the Messiah, in what is traditionally called 'the Magnificat' (Luke 1:46–55).

Becoming a parent changes our whole perspective on who we are. Our lives, ambitions and goals are no longer what they were. Before becoming a mum I had a career in media and public relations. I was ambitious and used to a fast-paced life with lots of travel. I measured success by my visible achievements, and my self-worth often came from what I did and what that represented. Although I was excited about becoming a mum, I knew that my new job title of 'full-time mum' would not be valued by everyone.

The fears I had about losing my labels stemmed from a false belief that these things made me who I was. I was afraid that motherhood would mean a loss of my dreams and a denial of who God had made me. But I am now discovering that my identity is rooted in what God thinks of me through Christ, not in any role or job title. Whether I am travelling around the world or rocking my baby to sleep, whether I am influencing thousands or influencing just the one precious life I have been given, I belong to God and am wholly loved by him.

We must hang on to our God-given dreams, but we may have to sacrifice some opportunities in order to make space for our children. Some ambitions may have to be put on hold; others may disappear completely, and new ambitions may come along. Our role may have changed, but our identity as children of God has not.

Be inspired by Mary. Her thankfulness and humility in a season of change shows us what a life of faith can look like. Can you begin to thank God for the new opportunities ahead of you? Can you humbly let go of your old labels and start to live fully in the here and now? A mother who knows who she is in Christ is certainly a world-changer, and will have a considerable influence on the lives of her children.

 Act and pray

Write down three of your ambitions in a journal. Listen to what God has to say about them. Is he asking you to lay down any of these dreams for now? Is he asking you to hold on to them? Is he giving you new ambitions? Share your thoughts with your spouse or a close friend and pray together.

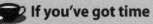 **If you've got time**

1. A powerful way to remind yourself of your identity as a child of God is to stand in front of the mirror and pray Scripture over yourself. Start with these verses and then add your own: Ephesians 2:8; 1 Peter 2:9; Romans 8:38–39.

2. Tear out a picture from a magazine or newspaper that represents your life before having your child. Thank God for the opportunities your old life brought. Put this picture away somewhere, using the following excerpt from a hymn as a prayer:

   Take my life, and let it be consecrated, Lord, to Thee.
   Take my moments and my days; let them flow in ceaseless praise.'[6]

3. Reread Mary's Magnificat in Luke 1:46–55. Write your own Magnificat or 'song to God', expressing your feelings about motherhood so far and the changes you are experiencing.

'Becoming a mum can unhinge everything. Roles and relationships are turned on their heads. Our career aspirations, plans for ministry, our hopes . . . all the things that have contributed to our sense of self are laid waste by the small human being who is now in our care. Babies care nothing for career plans . . . They just want our time and affection, someone to sing, food and sleep. It is mundane, exhausting and exhilarating and it requires our all. It never feels like our all is enough, but it is. Our broken, imperfect, tired, angry, frustrated, questioning, empty *all* is exactly what our babies need.'

Joy, mum to Isaac, ten, Caleb, eight, and Moses, one

Related to this theme:
Month 4, Week 4: A sense of self

Month 2: A Season of Change

Week 4: Patience in the storm

By Louie

Bring to mind a few mothers of young children whom you know and respect. What qualities do you admire in them? I hold in high esteem those who are really patient. On becoming a mum, I discovered how impatient I really was. Is the baby *still* crying? Do I need to feed you *again*? Not *another* load of washing . . .

Being with another human being almost twenty-four hours a day, seven days a week means that, even though we adore them to bits and want to be with them that much, it is tough to find the head space or prayer space we need to bring our emotions to God. As a consequence I often find myself lacking patience, and so being irritable and quick to become angry.

In 1 Corinthians we read:

> Love is patient, love is kind. It does not envy, it does not boast, it is not proud. It is not rude, it is not self-seeking, it is not easily angered, it keeps no record of wrongs. Love does not delight in evil but rejoices with the truth. It always protects, always trusts, always hopes, always perseveres. Love never fails.
> (1 Corinthians 13:4–8a)

This description perfectly encapsulates the nature and character of God. His love is the love I want to emulate to my husband and child and those around me. But I am challenged even to display the first characteristic on the list! I wonder which characteristic you sense God would like you to work on, as you seek to love those in your life.

The trouble with my impatience, and sometimes my anger, is that I can't express my feelings to my helpless baby. She can't talk it all through with me, and from me she just needs love and warmth. It isn't her fault that sometimes I find motherhood – and just life itself – a real battle. So often it's my husband or another 'safe' family member or friend who is unfortunate enough to feel the full force of my frustration. Many new parents recount that, while having a baby together is a wonderful thing for them, they also find themselves bickering as never before, as each channels the new stresses they are experiencing into the other.

Emotions are a wonderful thing – just imagine how boring life would be without them. Feeling angry or frustrated is not always wrong, but Paul teaches in Ephesians:

> 'In your anger do not sin': Do not let the sun go down while you are still angry.
> (Ephesians 4:26)

If God is impressing on your conscience that you have hurt him or others when angry, then you need to ask for forgiveness. This doesn't need to take long: if all that's available is a fleeting moment in which to say sorry to God, then seize the opportunity. Perhaps you could do this while you are in the shower, pushing the buggy or standing at the kitchen sink. If you are feeling far from God, you need only to come to him and say sorry for your mistakes, and you will be right back in his presence, cleansed and perfect before him once more.

Act and pray

As an act of prayer, write a letter to God, sharing your feelings, frustrations and struggles with him.

If you've got time

1. Meditate on the following verse and then invite God to speak calm into your spirit:

   He [Jesus] got up, rebuked the wind and said to the waves, 'Quiet! Be still!' Then the wind died down and it was completely calm.
   (Mark 4:39)

2. Look back to 1 Corinthians 13:4–8a. Read it aloud, replacing the word 'love' with your own name. Do this as a prayer for your love for others to become more and more like God's.

3. If you sense that God is calling you to repent, use Psalm 51 to help you do so:

Have mercy on me, O God,
  according to your unfailing love;
according to your great compassion
  blot out my transgressions . . .
Create in me a pure heart, O God,
  and renew a steadfast spirit within me.
(Psalm 51:1, 10)

'One of the things about new motherhood that took me by surprise was that I thought I was a patient person – but it turns out I am not! The daily accumulation of things not going as I had anticipated left me quite resentful towards our daughter. I had thought I would be a "natural" mum; however, I found that I had to work really hard at it.'

Alise, mum to Amelie, seven, and Isaac, five

Related to this theme:
Month 2, Week 2: A new family member

Month 3: Letting Go

Week 1: Gina Ford versus *The Baby Whisperer*

By Louie

I'll never forget the first time I opened a book on caring for a newborn baby. My mind was boggled after just a few pages. I was overwhelmed with information, and all I had learned about was what I needed to get hold of in order to set up a nursery.

Reading about baby care before you have the real version in your arms is a bit like studying a guide to playing tennis before you've held a racket. So, although I dipped into some books before our daughter arrived, it wasn't until after she was born that I really got stuck into the wisdom of Gina Ford and *The Baby Whisperer*, among others.[1]

Initially I felt deeply comforted by the thought that I had just picked up a comprehensive user manual for my child. But unfortunately my baby didn't seem to comply with the manual's instructions, and then things seemed more pear-shaped than ever. Whenever I tried to encourage her to follow a rigid timetable of feeding and sleeping, as some of the books suggested, I felt like a failure because we never reached the golden standard.

I have a tendency to be a perfectionist, and wanting to do the best for my baby seemed to give me licence to let my perfectionism run wild. But, in doing so, I began to trust in myself rather than God. Proverbs 3:5–6 reminds us:

> Trust in the LORD with all your heart
>   and lean not on your own understanding;
> in all your ways acknowledge him,
>   and he will make your paths straight.

Books on baby care can provide us with essential and much-needed guidance. But who are we more dependent on: the latest baby expert, or a God who answers prayer and provides us with all we need to love and raise our children? The more I read, the more there was to think about, as the baby experts offered me their range of opinions and ideas. Should I go down the demand-feeding or routine-feeding route, I wondered? Should I begin weaning at four months or six?

Gradually I came to realize that the diverse approaches of the experts reflect the diversity among our children. My responsibility is primarily to love my children, and to trust my God-given instinct to care for them well. In so doing, I am trusting in my Creator.

 **Act and pray**

Paul writes in Philippians 2:24: 'I am confident in the Lord.' Paul is self-confident – or sure of his own abilities – because he is sure of Christ living in him. Meditate on this sentence, repeating it aloud over and over again or silently as a prayer. Ask God to give you new confidence in your own parenting abilities. He is within you, giving you what you need.

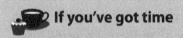 **If you've got time**

1. Do you struggle with perfectionism? Chris Ledger and Wendy Bray write on this subject:

   Perfectionism is usually a cycle: a veritable hamster wheel of perfectionist habits from which it is hard to escape . . . First, an unrealistic goal is set which raises expectations. Then, as soon as that goal is in place, we (if we are perfectionists) begin to fear either not meeting it at all or failing to meet it as and when we expected. We can start to live under a constant pressure to achieve, padding away constantly on the wheel in order to 'get it right' . . .[2]

   If you relate to this quotation, try to identify the latest unrealistic goal that you have set yourself. Bring this to God in prayer, asking him to show you why you feel the need to achieve this. Invite him to help you to let go of it, and to help you experience freedom instead of pressure.

2. What sort of literature, media and individuals are informing and influencing not only your parenting decisions, but also your wider thinking at the moment? Make a list or draw a spider diagram. Looking at this,

are you happy with the balance of input you are receiving? Is God challenging you to do something differently?

3. Use a 'palms-down, palms-up' prayer to invite God to be the centre of your parenting. Place your palms down as a symbol of your desire to submit to God, silently asking him to help you trust him. Then turn your palms up, symbolizing your desire to receive from the Lord. Ask for whatever you need at the moment as a mum.

'A lot of the early stages of motherhood are to do with confidence, trusting your own instincts, and praying. As a new mum, you can get overloaded with advice, but you simply need to break things down into the most basic details of life: eating, sleeping, exercising and loving.'

Carole, mum to Billy, eight months

 Related to this theme:
Month 3, Week 3: Embracing imperfection

Month 3: Letting Go

Week 2: Feeling alone

By Anna

> But I will sing of your strength,
>> in the morning I will sing of your love;
> for you are my fortress,
>> my refuge in times of trouble.
>
> (Psalm 59:16)

The Psalms give us a vocabulary with which to express our feelings to God. They are full of vulnerable, honest cries for help to the God who is not afraid of strong emotions, but welcomes our heartfelt prayers and is deeply concerned for our needs. David wrote this particular psalm at a time when his life was under threat and he was feeling desperate. King Saul had sent men to watch David's house in order to kill him.

Going through a time of change can cause a crisis within us, but it can also be the very place in which we encounter God. French philosopher Paul Ricoeur talks about change involving three stages: orientation, disorientation and reorientation. In the disorientation stage there is always a tension between 'the movement to cling to what has been lost as a source of a much-needed sense of belonging' and on the other hand, 'the ability to go out and grasp a revitalized identity in a new world'.[3]

For some people, the disorientation stage can manifest itself as post-natal depression, an illness that as many as 10% of all recently delivered women develop.[4] (See the profile on page 86 for an insight into one mum's experience of post-natal depression.) You may not have suffered from this, but may relate to the deep sense of isolation felt by a mum of an eight-month-old, who said, 'At around three months, my son had a painful tummy for a time, and I was up a lot at night. My husband gets up early for work, so it was only me doing the nights. I started to feel really lonely, which then makes you feel vulnerable, and if you aren't careful, angry towards your partner. I thought, "Why me? Why me, every single night?" Then it struck me that I wasn't alone. Jesus was always with me, and I could pray as much as I liked. He was always there, always listening. That was a really important part of my spiritual life, realizing that when I was up with my son, I could sing songs to him, both secular and spiritual. I could remember bits from worship songs, and Bible passages that I had read ages ago came to mind. I realized I wasn't in this on my own.'

If you suspect you are experiencing post-natal depression, then seek professional help.[5] If you aren't, you may still identify with feelings of isolation, fear and being out of control. It may be that, at this time, all you can do is cry out to God, as David did. Let God embrace you. Know that he is Emmanuel, 'God with us'. As Psalm 59 says, he is your fortress; your refuge in times of trouble.

Act and pray

God is not afraid of our feelings. He is not afraid of our tears. In fact, we know that Jesus himself wept with compassion when his friend Lazarus had died (John 11:35). Bring your raw emotions to God and know that he accepts you as you are. Write your own psalm to God, trying to be as honest as you can.

If you've got time

1. When you are feeling isolated, the Psalms can give voice to your emotions. You may want to read through the following psalms, written by David during some of the challenges he faced: Psalm 13; Psalm 38; and Psalm 143.

2. The Psalms were intended to be put to music. This week, play your favourite music, sing and worship God with your baby, in the middle of the chaos.

3. When we feel depressed we can often think that we are the only ones going through this experience. But we are not alone. There were many women who felt depressed in the Bible, such as Naomi (Ruth 1 – 2) and Hagar (Genesis 21:8–21). God used them mightily. Read their stories and look for the ways in which God brought hope into their lives.

'I was surprised that I felt so empty after the birth of our first child. We had spent such a long time waiting, praying and longing for a child to come along. I expected to feel jubilant and to praise God. But I almost felt the opposite – nothing at all. I did regain that sense of praise again, but in a different shape. I spent a lot of time walking and praying and listening. That was great because, for the first time ever, my faith integrated into every part of my life.'

Sam, mum to Charlie, three, Jessica, eighteen months, and twenty weeks pregnant

Related to this theme:
Month 1, Week 3: Light in the darkness

Month 3: Letting Go

Week 3: Embracing imperfection

By Louie

As Jesus was on his way, the crowds almost crushed him. And a woman was there who had been subject to bleeding for twelve years, but no-one could heal her. She came up behind him and touched the edge of his cloak, and immediately her bleeding stopped.

'Who touched me?' Jesus asked . . . 'I know that power has gone out from me.'

Then the woman, seeing that she could not go unnoticed, came trembling and fell at his feet. In the presence of all the people, she told why she had touched him and how she had been instantly healed. Then he said to her, 'Daughter, your faith has healed you. Go in peace.'

(Luke 8:42b–48)

'Don't worry about having a neat and tidy home – just let things go. This season is about you and your baby. Ignore the mess.'

A wave of frustration comes over me every time I hear this sort of advice, liberally doled out to mums of newborns. But why does it grate with me so much?

In the early months of motherhood, life suddenly seemed so outside my control. With every day so unpredictable, knowing that my home was in a respectable state gave me a reassuring sense that I had a handle on something in my world. I might have achieved little all day long, but at least I had made a dent in the laundry mountain.

When our home is well presented, we can feel as though we are this way within ourselves, and it can briefly lift our mood. But do we in fact want to hide what is going on inside with a lovely exterior, because we are not sure how to handle what or who might be lurking there?

The woman in the story above had been haemorrhaging for twelve years and felt shame at her condition. The way she makes a dash for Jesus, hoping she will be unseen (verse 44), indicates that she had grown accustomed to hiding her true self from others. But Jesus won't let her go 'unnoticed' any longer (verse 47). By publicly healing her, he not only restores her physically, but also restores her human dignity. Her fear of being noticed becomes the route by which Jesus performs the second part of the healing – he puts an end to her shame.

Sometimes, our unmasking can be our healing. During this past year I have begun to learn to let go of idealism over the state of my home, and instead to allow visitors to see that I am not 'on top' of everything in life.

Even now I can spot several enormous coffee stains on my living-room carpet that I haven't even begun to try to remove. I want humbly to invite others to see something more of the real me, stains and all.

Act and pray

Do an experiment with yourself and God this week. Ignore some housework, or leave your home in a real mess for a set period of time. (Perhaps warn your spouse you are doing this!) Does it feel as bad as you expected? Use the time that you would have spent on chores to read the Bible or pray.

During this prayer time you could:

- Reflect on Jesus' love for you as someone who is at times messy and far from perfect.

- Ask him to speak to you about how you are prioritizing your day-to-day time. When the baby sleeps, how much time is being allocated to housework? How much is being spent with God? In what ways could you bring God into the jobs you do around your home? Are there some jobs you could do less well in order to create more time for things with more significance?

If you've got time

1. Reflect on the following saying: 'If you look good on the outside, you'll feel good on the inside too.' To what extent does this reflect your philosophy, not only on how you keep your home but also on your personal appearance? What does God say to you about this? Look up Luke 12:31.

2. Take a prayer walk around your home. Instead of focusing on mess in each room, use what you see around you – pictures, photos, the view from a window – to inspire prayer.

3. Look up Mark 2:15–17. What sort of people did Jesus choose to hang out with? How is God calling you to respond to him now?

'When the kids were young, some mums had immaculate houses – everything was colour-co-ordinated, with matching crockery. I used to really covet it all. When my mother-in-law died we inherited some money, and suddenly we could have bought lots of things. But her death knocked our values into shape. God said to me that when I reach the pearly gates he is not going to ask me whether I vacuumed under the bed. There are far more important things in life than what your home looks like.'

Outi, mum to Tove, fifteen, Sanna, thirteen, and David, eleven

Related to this theme:
Month 3, Week 1: Gina Ford versus *The Baby Whisperer*

Month 3: Letting Go

Week 4: 'I feel like a bad mum'

By Anna

There's a saying that when a woman gives birth to a child she also gives birth to guilt. Not all guilt is bad. Sometimes the Holy Spirit draws attention to the things in our lives that are not pleasing God and gently brings his conviction. But motherhood can also bring an unhealthy false guilt about all kinds of things. Is it wrong to give my baby a bottle if I can't breastfeed? Do I leave my child too long to cry in his cot? Is she too dependent on a pacifier/dummy?

When my daughter was three months old, I was changing her nappy on a changing table in a restaurant and she suddenly began to shriek in pain. Panicked, my eyes scanned the surroundings and saw that the fingers of her right hand had got stuck in a sharp groove. I carefully freed her fingers, scooped her up and soothed her. Tears poured down my face as I felt her pain. I should have seen the potential danger, I thought. I felt incredibly guilty and angry at myself.

This was a relatively minor incident with no lasting damage, but sometimes we face big issues with our children that we are tempted to think of wrongly as 'our fault'. We can begin to see everything as our fault, and this doesn't form a healthy foundation for our parenting. I find great solace in this passage from Romans, where Paul says, 'Therefore, there is now no condemnation for those who are in Christ Jesus, because through Christ Jesus the law of the Spirit of life set me free from the law of sin and death' (Romans 8:1–2).

No condemnation! What an incredible blessing, given to us freely in Christ. Christ accepts us unconditionally. Christ forgives us unconditionally. Christ loves us unconditionally. Christ has given us freedom from our actual guilt as well as our false guilt through his death on the cross. Can we then begin to recognize ourselves as accepted, forgiven and loved no matter what mistakes we have made? This will lead the way to accepting, forgiving and loving our own children unconditionally as they grow older.

How can we begin to live in this freedom? I find it's easier in community. A first step may be to spend time with a friend who is happy in their own skin and helps you to feel relaxed in their presence. Contentment is a contagious characteristic and a great antidote to guilt.

Decide today to allow God to free you from the shackles of false guilt and shame. There's nothing too difficult for him.

 **Act and pray**

We can leave our guilt and shame at the cross of Christ. Find five minutes alone, and look for something around the house that has a cross symbol on it (a necklace, a picture, a Bible or an ornament) or draw a simple cross on a piece of paper. Sit somewhere comfortable and look at or hold the cross.

- Ask the Holy Spirit to show you where you have done things to displease God, but also where you have been carrying false guilt.

- Confess any sins the Holy Spirit draws attention to, and ask him to help you deal with the feelings of false guilt for things that are not your fault.

- Thank Jesus for declaring you 'not guilty' before him through his death on the cross, and ask him to help you live in contentment and freedom.

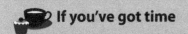 **If you've got time**

1. Angela Ashwin talks about praying with unlikely ingredients. This means praying with the very experiences that we had seen as blockages to our spiritual life.[6] If you become bogged down by guilty feelings during the week, use these feelings as unlikely ingredients and come to God in prayer. Try this while you are cooking.

2. . . . Return to the LORD your God,
     for he is gracious and compassionate,
     slow to anger and abounding in love . . .
     (Joel 2:13)

If there are things you have done which you cannot forget or for which you cannot accept Christ's forgiveness, then return to your gracious and compassionate Father. It may help to take steps towards talking and praying with a minister or counsellor.

3. Celebrating is a great way of counteracting the oppressive nature of false guilt and shame. Arrange a celebration of motherhood so far. Invite some friends over and thank God together for what he's done in you, asking him to fill you with the knowledge of his will for this next stage of parenting (Colossians 1:9).

'One of the things I struggle with as a new mother is that I constantly compare myself with other mums. Other babies never seem to cry . . . This is where a lie enters in: "You are doing this so wrong; you are such a bad mum." I have been learning to accept the truth that, through God's strength, I am a good mum, and that this doesn't change when Caitlin's having a rough day or I make a mistake.'

Lydia, mum to Caitlin, four months

Month 4: Relationship Shake-up

Week 1: Investing in your marriage

By Anna

When a baby comes along, existing relationships often end up taking a back seat. Less time to spend with others can mean that some friendships flounder, but for other relationships, a new baby can bring a surprising depth, intimacy and joy.

Before we had our first child, my husband, Azariah, and I asked a number of couples what they did to nurture their marriage during those early months of parenthood. One of my favourite tips was: 'Pray together, read together, laugh together, talk together, share moments together!' This advice helped us immensely, especially the bit about laughing.

One evening, Azariah and I were worn out after trying without success to get our daughter to sleep. She finally fell asleep, poised in mid-air, face down, with Azariah's hands on each side of her waist! We carefully laid her down on a pillow on the floor so as not to wake her, then each picked up one end of the pillow, attempting to manoeuvre her safely across to the Moses basket in our room. As Azariah bent down to pick the pillow up, we heard a loud *rrrriiiiiiip* and were horrified to see his cord trousers had split from front to back! Trying to suppress raucous laughter, prevent waking our baby and not drop the pillow was next to impossible. Enjoying this moment of joy together relieved a stressful situation and made us realize how much we missed laughing together. It gave us renewed strength to get through the week.

Laughter and having fun can be a great way to keep your marriage strong. We do not often associate joy and fun with holy living. Instead, we tend to think of them as superficial and not very spiritual.

In the book of Nehemiah, joy brings strength to the people. The prophet Nehemiah calls the people to enjoy a celebratory meal after they have completed the rebuilding of Jerusalem's walls, saying, ' . . . the joy of the Lord is your strength' (Nehemiah 8:10).

Joy that comes from God actually strengthens us, gives us a new lease of energy, bonds us in relationship with others and equips us for the task in hand. In this context, joy also enables the people to express generosity and repair their relationship with God, just as in our marriage joy can build bridges and bring healing.

If your marriage is strained because of your changing circumstances, spend some quality time with your spouse this week and talk about your relationship. How's your love life? If you haven't already done so, is this a good time to move the baby into his or her own room and enjoy some intimacy again?

Act and pray

Inject some joy into your marriage this week. What makes you and your spouse smile? Perhaps you could watch your favourite comedy DVD together, go on a date with friends who always make you laugh, or contact them on Skype. If time is short, you could watch snippets of your favourite comedian on YouTube. As you do so, thank God for his gifts of fun and joy and ask him to strengthen your marriage.

If you've got time

1. Erwin McManus, leader of the Mosaic church in California, asked: 'What if the most sacred experience in the world was a moment of unrestrained laughter?'[1] Reflect on the holiness of laughter this week and pay attention to the moments when God brings joy into your life.

2. 'The fruit of the Spirit is . . . joy' (Galatians 5:22). Eat a piece of fruit and use it as a trigger for prayer, asking God to help you to grow joy in your marriage.

3. Your baby may be beginning to smile and laugh by now. Each time he or she does so, pray a short prayer: 'Thank you, Lord, that your joy is my strength.'

'We have worked out a rhythm of life that allows for family time, marriage time, time alone digging into our spiritual pathways and time with others. Marriage time hasn't reduced, it just looks different: candle-lit meals at home (rather than out), movies in, hot baths and daytime dates. Sure, it requires a little bit more work, and some things may even come up that you have to deal with quickly, given the added responsibilities you now have, but it is completely realistic to have a contented marriage from which flows a contented family life. We muck up mightily, but are passionate about making it work better, and, with the Lord's help, we are all journeying and growing together.'

Sally, mum to Samuel, two, and Arabella, six months

Related to this theme:
Month 12, Week 2: Let's celebrate

Month 4: Relationship Shake-up

Week 2: Nurturing friendships

By Louie

When I reflect on my relationships with friends who had children before I did, I realize how totally inadequate I have been in supporting them through the baby-rearing season of their lives. Having babies of my own has shown me that my ability to be a good friend and enjoy friendships with others looks a little different when there is a young child, or indeed children, in the mix.

At the start of Jesus' ministry, he chose twelve men to be his disciples. They became a close-knit group of friends who learned from him and supported him in his divine mission (Luke 6:12–15). The Gospels also suggest that Jesus had three particularly close, special friends – Peter,

James and John – whom he often selected from among his followers to do things with (Mark 9:2).

Even Jesus, Saviour of the world, needed and nurtured a few deep, supportive friendships. However, a closer look at his relationship with Peter reveals that they had their ups and downs. In just one chapter of Matthew's Gospel, Peter oscillates from making a radical confession of Jesus as the Christ to trying to prevent Jesus from fulfilling God's call on his life. Jesus responds by strongly rebuking Peter.[2]

When Jesus is crucified, it is the same dear friend Peter who three times publicly denies having ever known him. What astounds me is Jesus' ability to forgive and continue to love his friend, even after such inconsistent behaviour. After his resurrection, Jesus publicly reinstates Peter, showing everyone present how he still loves and believes in him. In John's Gospel we read:

> When they had finished eating, Jesus said to Simon Peter, 'Simon son of John, do you truly love me more than these?'
> 'Yes, Lord,' he said, 'you know that I love you.'
> Jesus said, 'Feed my lambs.'
> (John 21:15)

How do you feel about your friendships at the moment? Perhaps you can relate to Peter, and know you have let others down. Perhaps you feel abandoned by old friends. Jenny, mum to Ella, twelve months, said, 'Relationships with friends – especially friends who don't have babies – have changed since I became a mum. I thought that friends I had known for the past ten years would be really interested in Ella, but I have felt that people without children haven't made the time to visit . . . I don't really see how things will change with these friends until they start having children. I just have to accept things as they are.'

If your friends haven't supported you as you had hoped, bring your disappointment to God, and ask him to help you forgive as Jesus did Peter. Is God asking you to invest more deeply in fewer friends? Or there may be new friendships that he is calling you to. I have found it hugely valuable to build relationships with a group of Christian mums of pre-school children, with whom I regularly meet to share the joys and pains of motherhood, seek God and pray together.

Act and pray

Inviting God to speak to you, write down the names of three friends: one you want to thank God for, another you feel let down by and need to forgive, and another who you know needs prayer. Use this list to help you pray for these three friends this week.

If you've got time

1. Send a text or email including an encouraging Bible verse to those three friends. You could also arrange to meet one of them for coffee, deciding before you go that, while you are together, you will affirm and build them up. Ask God if there is anything specific he would like you to say to them, or a Bible verse you could share.

2. Look up Colossians 1:9–13. This is Paul's prayer for his friends in the church at Colossae. Read these verses slowly, holding a particular friend in mind as you do so and using Paul's words to inspire prayer.

3. What kind of friend would you like to be to others? Write down three qualities that you value in your friends and ask God to help you develop these characteristics.

'Once I arrived at our mums' group half an hour late – flustered, crying and at the end of my tether with a screaming child. I was welcomed as if I were the Queen. I experienced blessing in every way, and by the end of the morning I could say with integrity, "God is good", something I had totally lost sight of. It was a moment when I was truly broken, exposed and vulnerable, and the Lord led me to a place of safety, restoration and hope. I was reminded that receiving as well as giving causes us to grow in maturity and faith. God was teaching me that it is good to be weak, for he will be strong. He has more resources than I can imagine.'

Alise, mum to Amelie, seven, and Isaac, five

Month 4: Relationship Shake-up

Week 3: A new season with your parents

By Anna

Staying at my parents' house for a week with my four-month-old daughter brought back some unexpected childhood memories of my relationship with my own mum.

I was sleeping in my childhood bedroom, and my daughter was sound asleep in her travel cot beside me. I remembered lying in this same bed as a girl, having had an argument with my mum and feeling that my parents didn't understand me. I also recalled as a teenager sitting up in bed and having late-night chats with mum about boyfriends and which of my girlfriends had fallen out with which and why. I remembered lying awake at night as an older teenager, wondering if I would ever meet the man of my dreams and become a mum myself. That world seemed such a long way away. And now it was here.

Having a baby, whether for the first time or not, can give rise to challenging problems with your parents and in-laws. I remember feeling annoyed with my mum during my pregnancy for being so obsessed with my health, but in hindsight I realize she was exhibiting the same protective instinct that I demonstrate towards my own daughter.

I've spoken to so many mums who have exclaimed with surprise, 'I keep doing things that my mum did when I was little. I'm turning into her!' I too recognize in myself as a mother a lot of traits that I see in my own mum – some good and some not so good. I realize that I need to exhibit grace to myself as well as my to own mother, as I hope my daughter will one day show grace towards me.

Perhaps motherhood has brought you closer to your parents and in-laws as you care for the baby together. Many fragmented families come together when a baby is born, forgetting past hurts in order to celebrate new life. Sally, mum of two, said, 'My relationship with my mother has changed for the better since I became a mother myself. I understand her much more, and she me. Our relationship is now flourishing into something beautiful, something to be celebrated.'

Our relationship with our parents matters to God. The only commandment given to Moses that comes with a promise concerns our attitudes towards our parents: 'Honour your father and your mother, so that you may live long in the land the Lord your God is giving you' (Exodus 20:12).

What does it mean to honour your parents in this phase of life? Perhaps your parents weren't very honourable when you grew up. Perhaps they were even physically or emotionally absent. In practice, honouring them now could mean refusing to get angry if they offer unneeded advice. Perhaps honouring means giving them space and opportunity to enjoy their new grandchild. If your parents weren't around during your childhood, who were those older role models for you? Choose to involve them in this adventure of motherhood.

As you honour your parents, you can be sure that you are modelling for your child something that you hope they will reciprocate in the coming years.

 Act and pray

Find some family photograph albums. Use the photos to pray and thank God for the legacy of traditions, values, culture and stories that your parents and grandparents have left you. Find a photograph of your baby. Pray for the legacy that you and your partner will one day leave him or her, and that it would establish a good foundation of faith.

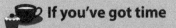 **If you've got time**

1. Read Luke 2:41–52 about Jesus' relationship with his own parents. Imagine you are Jesus' parents in the story. What are some of your emotions and thoughts? Ask God to give you insight into your own parents' feelings at this time.

2. Families can often give unwanted advice about how to bring up children. If you've been struggling with a particular relationship, write a letter

to that person about how you're feeling, and use it as a prayer, even if you never send it.

3. Honour your parents and in-laws by celebrating their becoming grand-parents. Do something special, such as sending them a framed photo of your baby with a thank-you card.

'The hardest thing about having a baby was figuring out my relationship with my family. I have eleven brothers and sisters, and we are very close. It was tough working out my identity in relationship to them. My mum only ever offered advice when I asked for it, but still I wondered what she would think every time I made a decision about Mercy. How long should I breastfeed? When should I put her in her own room? I had to keep saying to myself, "You're an adult. You can decide yourself."'

Yolanda, mum to Mercy, two, and Solomon, five weeks

Related to this theme:
Month 10, Week 4: Reflecting on your own childhood

Month 4: Relationship Shake-up

Week 4: A sense of self

By Louie

> Do you not know that your body is a temple of the Holy Spirit, who is in you,
> whom you have received from God?
>
> (1 Corinthians 6:19)

I recently read an article in the *Daily Telegraph* which began: 'Women are under pressure from [the example of] celebrity mothers to lose their baby weight rapidly after giving birth . . . '[3] This isn't new information: we are all aware of the media's depiction of flawless female beauty, and the influence of an unattainable standard offered by celebrity culture. With this comes the unrealistic expectation that we should look a picture of radiance and health, even immediately after childbirth, and in the early months of motherhood.

For most mothers of young babies, the matter of your post-partum body is no small one. In the first few months following both my children's births, my body looked and functioned nothing like it had done before. I was leaky and saggy and my hair fell out. On the one hand, I was so busy with my family that I didn't have much time to dwell on my appearance, and just tried to live as normally as I could with a sore and healing body. On the other, I avoided facing my feelings about myself, as when your body is in this sort of state it can be hard to love and accept yourself.

The verse above says that your body is God's dwelling place. The Holy Spirit lives within your physical form, regardless of your condition. How are you currently thinking about your body? What sorts of words, phrases and feelings come to your mind when you look in the mirror?

Do you feel disgusted? Remember, God loves you as you are.

Do you feel ashamed? Remember, God created you to carry and bear a baby. He is delighted with what you have allowed your body to do.

Do you wish you were different? Ask God to help you love yourself in your current physical state.

1 Corinthians 6:19–20 says: 'You are not your own; you were bought at a price. Therefore honour God with your body.' How can you honour God with your body at this moment? Do you need to ask him to help you to love a flawed physique, and choose to see the beauty in what he

has made? Is it time to start eating more sensibly or taking some gentle exercise? Do you need to ask someone to cook you some meals, so that you can eat well instead of skipping meals when you are caring for your baby? Perhaps, for you, honouring God with your body means prioritizing him over your appearance. Proverbs 31:30 says: 'Charm is deceptive, and beauty is fleeting; but a woman who fears the LORD is to be praised.'

 Act and pray

Write down 1 Corinthians 6:19–20 on a piece of coloured card or sticky note, and put it in a spot where you will notice it regularly. I keep a verse card by my kitchen sink, on my bedside table and in my purse. When you see it, read it as a prayer, aloud or silently. You might also like to make verse cards using Jeremiah 1:5 or 1 Peter 3:3–4.

If you've got time

1. Talk to a friend who has had a child about the impact of childbirth on her body and sense of self-esteem. Which Bible verses helped her see God's truth during this time? Ask her to pray with you about your self-image.

2. Pamper yourself in a small way that helps build your body confidence this week. Paint your nails, enjoy a luxurious bubble bath or find someone to take your baby for an hour or two so that you can have a beauty treatment. As you do so, thank God for your whole body: the parts you like most and the parts that you are more self-conscious about.

3. If you are doing regular pelvic floor exercises, why not incorporate prayer into this activity? Try repeating sections of this verse as you work through your exercises: 'Heal me, O LORD, and I will be healed; save me and I will be saved, for you are the one I praise' (Jeremiah 17:14).

'It's thirteen months since Skye was born, and my body is still not functioning normally as my pelvic floor muscles were badly damaged in the process of giving birth. I have to avoid impact exercise and do endless pelvic floor exercises. I feel ashamed. My body is letting me down. I am running out of hope that it will right itself. It's a struggle to believe the truth of Psalm 139, that I am "fearfully and wonderfully made".'

Diary entry by Louie van der Hart, when Skye was thirteen months old

Related to this theme:
Month 2, Week 3: Identity shift

Profile of a mum

Focus: Post-natal depression

I had post-natal depression for four months after my first baby, Jonathan, was born. My overwhelming feeling was one of fear. Everyone had told me I would feel pleased when I had him, and that was what I had anticipated. I felt guilty because I thought I should feel happy, but instead I felt afraid. That made me feel isolated and alone.

Getting ready to go out with a baby is hard, but when you're depressed it's even harder. I didn't leave the flat for eight weeks. I just couldn't get myself together. When I did go out, people would see my baby and say, 'Ah, isn't he beautiful?! You must feel so happy.' But I didn't, and I couldn't admit it. I wanted to scream, 'You've no idea how awful it is!'

I was scared I was going to hurt my baby. Sometimes I would give him to my husband and say, 'You've got to take him.' I felt out of control. I felt guilty because I knew I should love my baby. I begged God to change my feelings for him.

The hardest thing was coming face to face with parts of myself I didn't know existed, and never would have guessed were there. I was used to being in control of my emotions. I discovered a very human part of myself. I'm a very competent, able person – to discover that base part of myself was important. It transformed me and my ministry. God met me in my weakness.

The worst thing somebody ever said to me at the time was, 'Are you reading your Bible?' It was devastating. All I could do was cry out to God. I was living off the fat – by that I mean that all I had stored up spiritually beforehand was there to sustain me in this dark time. There are times when we just need to live off the fat. There are times when God embraces us. I just used to curl up and ask God to pull me out of these depths. I couldn't do anything for myself.

The Psalms kept me going, but only because I knew them, and they were part of my vocabulary. I came back to them again and again. They were the only things raw and real enough – it was their immediacy. When you're going through post-natal depression you want to talk and sing and shout and scream. It's a terrifying place to be.

The most helpful thing people could do for me was the practical stuff. I'll never forget when our vicar's wife came round and said, 'You sleep. I'll look after Jonathan.' When I woke up, she had cleaned our kitchen. What a gift of grace. It was a spiritual thing she did. I remember being at theological college, and someone who was talking about Jesus' washing of the disciples' feet asked, 'What does it mean to wash feet?' I said, 'It means cleaning my oven', and everyone laughed. They didn't understand, but I truly meant what I said.

Lis, mum to Jonathan and Nell, now teenagers

Month 5: Fearfully and Wonderfully Made

Week 1: Finding treasure

By Louie

Since I had a child, countless more experienced parents have advised me: 'Enjoy every minute of the baby years – they whizz by! Before you know it, your newborn is a toddler, your toddler a teenager, and your teenager is flying the nest . . .'

Sometimes the days at home with my daughter pass incredibly slowly, and that advice is hard to believe. And then I watch her as she gradually reaches each developmental milestone, and I realize that it won't be long before the dependent-newborn phase is behind us. I feel a pang of melancholy that I will never see her like that again, and only have the memories to remind me.

In the second chapter of Luke's Gospel, we find his version of Jesus' birth story, and his account of Mary's unique experience of becoming a mother. Hidden away here is a little verse that hints at her approach to early motherhood: 'But Mary treasured up all these things and pondered them in her heart' (Luke 2:19).

Ruth, a mum of three, says, 'As a woman I have always identified with this verse; with Mary's quiet "treasuring" – her storing-up of moments of love, mystery, wonder and tenderness. These are moments that live on in my heart and memory, defining my life, shaping my soul. How much more so since becoming a mother! How much richer my treasure since the birth of my child?

The first flutters of her tiny limbs inside me.

The pride I felt in the roundness and tautness of my belly as she grew and grew.

The strength and determination of my body in labour, to bring this life into the world.

The surprise of her hot, red body and captivating cry as she burst into the world.

The sight of her nestled against my breast, feeding, sleeping, flesh from my flesh, skin to skin.

These moments are treasures. We will know them only once, or for a short time, and then they are gone. And so we go over and over them in our memories to preserve their sweetness.'

How can we become a little more reflective and thoughtful, savouring the riches and beauty of all that God has put into our lives, as Mary did? When one of my friends was feeling really under the weather with the stresses of new motherhood, her vicar's wife went to visit her. This wise lady's advice to her was gloriously simple: 'Slow everything down.'

Are you about to rush on to the next thing? Slow life down. Acknowledge the uniqueness of the season. Today, notice and treasure the precious moments, cherishing them in God's presence.

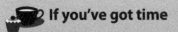 **Act and pray**

Ponder on the precious moments you have had with your baby – the things that brought a tear of joy, a spontaneous smile, or laughter shared with others. Thank God for these times. Is there a way that you could record them, so you can remember them in the future?

Now reflect on the treasure God has brought into your world through other relationships, your church or work. Thank him for these things too.

If you've got time

1. Look up Bible verses that teach us about treasure: Matthew 13:44; Mark 10:21; Matthew 6:20–21; and Psalm 19:7–9. What things does God see as precious? What does he want us to hold in high esteem, and teach our children to value?

2. Allow your ears to hear some precious nuggets of truth this week. You could tune in to a Christian radio station (for ideas, see the Resources

section on page 228), or worship God by meditating on the lyrics to some Christian music.

3. If you are starting to spend more time away from your baby – perhaps at work – stick some photos by your desk to remind you of the special moments God has given you with your child. Use these images as a reminder to thank God for your baby, and to pray for your unique relationship with him or her.

'Meditation – the "treasuring" of beautiful, strengthening thoughts – has been a source of sustenance to me since becoming a mother. It is a secret place, a retreat, a wellspring of strength for the times of pain, fear or exhaustion. Peace comes at 4 am, when, rising to feed a sick, comfortless child for the third time, you can dwell on the treasure of a plump, flushed cheek finding solace pressed against your own pale, thin, tired one. So when you need a retreat, spend time among your treasures in thanksgiving. Even if some of these experiences are bittersweet, and bring tears as well as smiles, invite God to be present in your pondering. Allow him to add to your heart's treasure store the jewels he reveals in his Word.'

Ruth, mum to Isla, five, Carys, two, and Keira, six months

 Related to this theme:
Month 7, Week 4: Through your baby's eyes

Month 5: Fearfully and Wonderfully Made

Week 2: Getting to know your baby

By Anna

Stop for a moment. If your baby is nearby, put him or her on your lap and take one of their hands. Turn the palm upwards and look closely at the intricate lines. Stroke their tiny fingers and observe the nails, knuckles and texture of the skin. What a beautiful creation your baby is! And it is not just their physical being that is intriguing. Watching your child's character unfold and wondering what kind of person they will be as they grow up is equally enthralling.

> Oh yes, you shaped me first inside, then out;
> you formed me in my mother's womb.

> I thank you, High God – you're breathtaking!
>> Body and soul, I am marvelously made!
>> I worship in adoration – what a creation!
> (Psalm 139:13–14, *The Message*)

Psalm 139 is a wonderful reminder of how special each child is to God. He has carefully made your baby's body and soul, and even saw them before they were fully formed (verse 16). We may only be beginning to discover their personality, but God knows them completely (verses 1–2).

When she was five months old I was really bonding with my daughter as she began to interact with toys and recognize me. Sometimes this 'enjoying the moment' can be spoilt when we concentrate on what milestones our child has or has not reached. Some parents begin to worry when their child is developing at a seemingly slower rate than other children. For others, there is the temptation to be competitive about their child's 'achievements'.

I discovered this when I began meeting with the group of mums who had attended my antenatal class – two hours of anxious mummies, screaming babies and a lot of drinking tea. Thursday mornings turned into coos of, 'Oooh, look at Bella's head control at only three weeks!' and 'Oh, Charlie's crying because he's teething three months early.'

Some friends of ours challenged me when they said they had decided not to tell other parents what their son was doing at each stage, as every child develops at a different rate. They were right. Inevitably, we miss the beautiful uniqueness of our child's development if we concentrate on 'milestones' and 'targets'.

Psalm 139 is not only a reminder of our child's uniqueness, but it also draws attention to the truth that our children are gifts to us. If we concentrate on their 'gifts', we often miss the fact that their whole lives are gifts! If your child has a disability or was born prematurely, then they may not be reaching the same milestones as other babies. Can you thank God for the gift of their lives in the midst of this challenge and resist the temptation to compare them with others?

To trust God with the development of our child means truly celebrating how fearfully and wonderfully they have been made. One of the joys of bringing up a child is to discover, day by day, their God-given aptitudes, appetites and mannerisms. Perhaps they have Granny's frown and Auntie Jane's eyebrows, Daddy's smile and Mummy's sociability. This is an opportunity to marvel at God's creativity – the God who created the universe has handcrafted your baby to perfection.

Act and pray

Go for a walk with your baby and, as you are walking, thank God for the unique characteristics you see developing in your child. Pray about how you can nurture those traits. You may also want to write down in a journal what kind of person you think your child will be when they're older.

If you've got time

1. Your child's name and family history are unique. If your child's name was chosen for its meaning, or if he or she is named after a family member or friend with particular characteristics, use this as a trigger for prayer.

2. Make a simple time capsule by putting some of your baby's favourite things, such as an old toy or a photo of a special time, into a shoebox. Keep the box as a reminder to pray for your child's developing character and preferences.

3. If you struggle with comparing your baby with other babies, share this with someone you trust. Give this person permission to ask you regularly how you are doing in this area.

'I loved seeing Eleanor's personality unfurl gradually. Every week there would be something new to marvel at, whether it was new things she was doing or just another facet becoming apparent of who she was. I'm so glad it happens this way – it gives you time to get used to having a child and helps you really to enjoy and appreciate who they are.'

Emma, mum to Eleanor, two, and Jemima, six months

 Related to this theme:
Month 7, Week 1: The power of story

Month 5: Fearfully and Wonderfully Made

Week 3: God with you through your child's suffering

By Louie

I waited patiently for the LORD;
    he turned to me and heard my cry.
He lifted me out of the slimy pit,
    out of the mud and mire;
he set my feet on a rock
    and gave me a firm place to stand.
He put a new song in my mouth,
    a hymn of praise to our God.
Many will see and fear
    and put their trust in the LORD.
(Psalm 40:1–3)

Perhaps one of life's slimiest, muddiest pits is experienced when your child is unwell and suffering pain. I have longed for my babies to be able to tell me exactly what is hurting, so that I don't have to play the guessing game of wondering what I should do to help them. Susie, mum of two, said, 'When one of my children is in pain, all I want to do is get them out of it. I drop everything, and just focus on trying to put an end to the pain, and comforting them. Everything else has to go out of the window.'

Psalm 40 affirms that when we cry out to God during difficult times he hears and comes to help us (verse 1). But when responding to a sick or teething baby, the practical can so quickly overwhelm us, and we can forget to call out to our Father. Susie says, 'It's so easy to forget to pray in those situations. But prayer needs to be my first stop. That brings peace. I try to remind myself that my baby is in God's hands, and if I love and care for my child, how much more so does God.'

In the verses above, the psalmist tells how God lifts him out of the muddy pit, firmly planting his feet upon the rock of security and safety that God alone can be (verse 2). As he sees God do this, he begins to thank him with infectious praise that causes others to see and trust in God too (verse 3). The psalmist later acknowledges that God has taught him new things through the trials he has faced – his 'ears have been pierced' (verse 6).

Dietrich Bonhoeffer, a pastor martyred during the Second World War for his opposition to the Nazis, wrote: ' . . . it is good to learn early that suffering and God are not contradictions, but rather a necessary unity . . . I believe that God is closer to suffering than to happiness, and that finding God in this way brings peace and repose and a strong, courageous heart.'[1]

 **Act and pray**

Use the two verses below from Psalm 40 as a prayer for yourself and for your child. In order to pray for your child, use their name where the psalmist uses the word 'me'.

> Do not withhold your mercy from me, O LORD;
>> may your love and your truth always protect me . . .
>
> Be pleased, O LORD, to save me;
>> O LORD, come quickly to help me.
>
> (Psalm 40:11, 13)

If you've got time

1. Look up the story of Jesus and Jairus' daughter in Luke 8:40–42 and 49–56. This highlights Jesus' power as the promised Messiah, and his mastery of death. What does it also teach you about Jesus' response to a sick child? How does it affect your faith in his intervention when your child is unwell?

2. Ask God to give you compassion for other children who are suffering. This week, as you read or watch the news, pray for children and families dealing with physical pain or challenging times. To help inspire your prayers, cut out stories from the newspaper featuring children who are suffering at the moment.

3. You might like to use the following prayer, written in the Celtic tradition:

> O Christ of the road
> of the wounded

O Christ of the tears
of the broken
In me and with me
the needs of the world
Grant me my prayers
of loving and hoping
Grant me my prayers
Of yearning and healing.[2]

'The most dramatic low I experienced during the first year of my daughter's life was at her eight-week check, when the doctor could not get a light reflex from her left eye. For two days we underwent specialist tests to see if it was a brain tumour. It turned out to be a rare single cataract. We were immensely thankful and thrilled that God was not going to take our beautiful, smiley baby away again so soon – but then we had to deal with the tension of "disappointed" grandparents who were upset that our little girl was not "perfect" and would never be able to see properly out of her left eye. We couldn't help but feel a bit angry, since to us she is "perfect" – just the way God intended her to be. Most people don't realize she doesn't use her left eye, and her eyes are a beautiful, deep blue-grey colour.'

Katy, mum to Aurora, ten months

Related to this theme:
Month 1, Week 2: The God who watches over us

Month 5: Fearfully and Wonderfully Made

Week 4: God working in your child's life

By Anna

> . . . we will tell the next generation
> the praiseworthy deeds of the LORD,
>   his power, and the wonders he has done.
> (Psalm 78:4)

I made my first conscious commitment to God when I was four and a half years old, marked by the three-inch letters scrawled at the front of my children's Bible: 'I asked Jesus into my heart today.' God was at work in my life, even before I could fully articulate it. My family and church community had also taken their responsibility seriously, as the Psalm above says, to 'tell the next generation the praiseworthy deeds of God'.

When our children are young, it is difficult to know how we can encourage the faith they may go on to have. Liz, mum to Toby, aged two, found two ways of doing this: 'Taking Toby up for Communion for a blessing when he was born was a key moment for me. I was almost in tears the first time.' She goes on to say, 'I also think it's important to pray with your child from an early age. We do simple prayers at bedtime now he's two. I leave a gap so Toby can pray for anything he wants. He'll usually say "Thank you for Daddy and teddies"!'

God's desire is for the whole community of faith to teach our child his loving commandments by embodying them:

> Love the LORD your God with all your heart and with all your soul and with all your strength. These commandments that I give you today are to be upon your hearts. Impress them on your children. Talk about them when you sit at home and when you walk along the road, when you lie down and when you get up. Tie them as symbols on your hands and bind them on your foreheads. Write them on the door-frames of your houses . . .
> (Deuteronomy 6:5–9)

The Israelite community were called to demonstrate to their children practically, and tell them regularly, what it meant to serve Yahweh. Your child's journey of faith won't just be influenced by whether or not you take them to church or pray with them, but also by the way in which the wider church family welcomes them.

Many people decide to have a thanksgiving, dedication or baptism service and/or to appoint godparents in order to welcome their child into the church family. We decided to incorporate a concept called the 'Life Village' into our daughter's baptism ceremony. The idea came from our observation that different parts of the world emphasize the benefit of extended family, summed up in the African proverb: 'It takes a village to raise a child.'

We asked a number of people of varying backgrounds, ethnicities, personalities and abilities to invest in our daughter's life in a specific way over her lifetime. Some offered to teach her skills like sewing or business, while others offered to take her on holidays or to give her the gift of quality time so that she can reach her God-given potential. These people were present at her baptism, and it was a powerful symbol of God's family welcoming our child.

We don't know when or whether our children will express their faith. Our responsibility is to love God with all that we are, and to surround them with loving Christian community, praying that one day they will love God with all their heart, soul and strength, and will be empowered to take the truth of that relationship into a world in need.

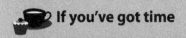 **Act and pray**

Prayerfully write down a simple message of encouragement for your child to read at the age of five, ten and fifteen. Put each message into a separate envelope and, on the corresponding birthday, give it to your child. You may want to do this with your spouse, or as a group activity at your child's thanksgiving, dedication or baptism service.

If you've got time

1. When your baby is having a bath, pray for every part of his or her body. For example, that their knees would learn the value of prayer and their ears would be tuned to God's voice.

2. Look back to Deuteronomy 6:9, and the instruction to write God's commands on the door-frames of your houses. If your child has a room of their own, create a card or picture incorporating a Bible verse and hang it on their wall.

3. What is the one characteristic of God that you want your child to grow up to know deeply? Using this as inspiration, pray for and with your baby at bedtime.

'Your child belongs to God. Ultimately they are on loan, and God is watching out for them. It is not all about you. The more people you have investing in and praying for you and your child, the better.'

Alise, mum to Amelie, seven, and Isaac, five

 Related to this theme:
Month 9, Week 3: Mum and evangelist

Month 6: Re-establishing Life Patterns

Week 1: Taking stock

By Anna

'How are you?' a friend asked me as I sat down with her for coffee one day when Eliana was six months old. I paused. Did she mean physically, emotionally, financially, relationally, spiritually or perhaps even ecologically?! I didn't know where to start. Everything had changed in six months. There were new routines, an often purely functional relationship with my husband, and on some days my biggest achievement was producing twenty pots of puréed vegetables. It was time to take stock.

So, how are you?

- First, think about your relationship with God since month one. Has it changed? Have you explored new ways of connecting with God? What's been your response to spiritually dry times?

- Now consider your relationship with your spouse. Are you enjoying parenting together and are you communicating honestly? How have you dealt with resentment? In the midst of tiredness, are you creating space for physical intimacy? If you are parenting alone, are you getting the help you need?

- Lastly, how are you adjusting to a constantly changing routine? As a new mum, I found it frustrating that, as soon as Eliana and I had got into a good rhythm, she would have a growth spurt or change her sleeping pattern, leaving me to play catch-up! If you are back at work, how are you managing the transition and increased demands?

Do you remember the spiritual ambitions you had when you were pregnant? At six months I was disappointed with myself for not maintaining the discipline of prayer for Eliana that I had begun in month one. But I knew that Jesus was with me on this journey and was able to meet me where I was.

> Now that same day two of them were going to a village called Emmaus, about seven miles from Jerusalem. They were talking with each other about everything that had happened. As they talked and discussed these things with each other, Jesus himself came up and walked along with them; but they were kept from recognising him.
> (Luke 24:13–16)

This is the story of Jesus meeting two of the disciples on the road to Emmaus after his death and resurrection. They think he is still dead, but he meets them in their grief and disappointment. They don't recognize him at first. But, as Jesus opens the Scriptures and later breaks bread, he is revealed to them. This encounter with Jesus transforms and empowers them.

Ask Jesus to reveal himself to you. Are you where you expected to be at this stage? Begin to entrust God with those areas of your life that need his transformation.

 Act and pray

It's time for a stocktake. If there is a specific time in the week when you do your admin jobs such as paying bills or sending emails, then use some of that time to include God in carefully considering the following three areas:

1. Your devotional life
2. Your marriage or close relationships
3. Your daily or weekly routine

Pray about these areas, asking God to speak to you. Thank him for walking with you on your journey so far, and ask him to prepare you for the next six months.

If you've got time

1. Many mums say that God is often harder to find with a baby around, but that the joy is greater when you do find him. Has this been your experience so far?

2. Physical intimacy is an important part of a healthy marriage. Gary Chapman in his book *Toward a Growing Marriage* lists suggestions that

wives have made to husbands about how to make sex more meaningful, such as: 'Take more of the responsibility for getting the children settled so that I can relax and spend more of the evening with you', and suggestions from husbands for wives, like: 'Do not say no too often.'[1] This week, talk and pray with your spouse about intimacy.

3. When your baby's pattern changes and throws you into confusion, repeat aloud the psalm below, asking God to guide you through the next phase:

> Turn your ear to me,
>   come quickly to my rescue;
> be my rock of refuge,
>   a strong fortress to save me.
> Since you are my rock and my fortress,
>   for the sake of your name lead and guide me.
> (Psalm 31:2–3)

'In the first year of motherhood I learnt that God is patient, and his love for us is truly, inconceivably big. Having a relationship with him is like a human relationship, in that it grows from season to season. He is forgiving. I thought I knew this already, but I know it even more now! I have felt incredibly inadequate over the last year, and yet I have also felt more accepted and loved by God.'

Hazel, mum to Zephan, eight months

 Related to this theme:
Month 12, Week 1: Reflecting on the past year

Month 6: Re-establishing Life Patterns

Week 2: Time for time out

By Louie

I wake up to silence. Immediately I wonder whether my daughter is OK, as my home is rarely quiet at 8 am. And then I remember: I'm on holiday in Italy, and she's back in the UK with my parents.

If you have already been on holiday with your baby, you won't need me to tell you that it's a very different experience from going away without one. For me, holidays taken with my children during their early years fell into one of two categories. Either I came home more exhausted than before we left, feeling disappointed that I hadn't had the break I had been longing for, or I felt energized and rested for the first time in weeks, and then plunged back into life at home with unsustainable verve. Before long

I'd run out of steam, and be forced to take seriously the concept of pacing myself.

The Bible's first reference to 'rest' comes in Genesis 2:2: 'By the seventh day God had finished the work he had been doing; so on the seventh day he rested from all his work.'

The pressures of new parenthood can leave us feeling that creating space in our lives for real rest is just another thing on the 'to-do list', only to be considered once everything else is complete. But if our Creator needed a break after six days' work, then we too need to take the idea of time out seriously. How and when we do this varies from person to person. I know mums of three-year-olds who have never left their children overnight, and others who went away for girlie weekends without their six-month-old babies. Perhaps for you, time out at the moment would simply mean a few hours of quality time spent on your own, with your spouse or with a close friend.

Jesus regularly left the crowds who followed him to rest in the presence of his Father and talk to him (see Mark 1:34–36). Do you need to ask God today to show you when – and perhaps even how – to rest again in this season of life?

Act and pray

Take a long, restful bath this week. If possible, find a time when your baby is sleeping and your home is quiet. A silent environment can help us to still our hearts before God, especially when we are accustomed to constant background noise. As you relax in the water, simply focus on being still in God's presence. Meditate on this verse: 'Be still, and know that I am God' (Psalm 46:10).

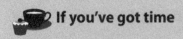 **If you've got time**

1. St Augustine wrote:

> God is delight
> and we rest in delight in Him,
> called home from the noise that is around us
> to the joys that are silent.

   This week, when you encounter a moment of silence in your day – even if it is a very short one – thank God for it. Allow yourself to take a tiny breather, and for a few moments 'rest in delight in him'.

2. Spend time talking to God about the rest you are currently getting. If you feel it is lacking, or you struggle to relax, ask him to provide you with the down time you need, and to speak to you about why you find it hard to wind down. In Matthew's Gospel, Jesus promises to show us how to rest:

> Are you tired? Worn out? Burned out on religion? Come to me. Get away with me and you'll recover your life. I'll show you how to take a real rest. Walk with me and work with me – watch how I do it. Learn the unforced rhythms of grace. I won't lay anything heavy or ill-fitting on you. Keep company with me and you'll learn to live freely and lightly.
> (Matthew 11:28–30, *The Message*)

3. Plan a time of rest – or a longer, restful holiday, if your situation allows it.

'When you go away on holiday as a parent of young children, you have to put things in place to make sure you have a rest. When my husband and I went away with the baby, we would go out and do things in the morning, and try to be back for her lunchtime sleep when we would read and just be together. We tried to carve out that time each day for ourselves. You need to accept that life is not the same, it's just not. And then try to enjoy what you do have. We do things like taking lots of photographs – celebrating what we have, now that we are a family. Celebrating the moment is important.'

Susie, mum to Jed, four, and Lily, fourteen months

 Related to this theme:
Month 6, Week 4: What's your maths?

Month 6: Re-establishing Life Patterns

Week 3: A hospitable home

By Anna

Jesus clearly loved food. There are so many stories in the Gospels where food is involved: the feeding of the five thousand (Luke 9:10–17), the Last Supper (Mark 14:12–26) and the fish barbecue on the beach (John 21:1–14), for example. Imagine you are having Jesus round for dinner. What would you cook? Would you serve up your most impressive meal and expensive wine? Would you rush to get the house spotless before he arrived?

When Jesus visited Peter's home, it led to a rather unusual dinner party. Jesus saw Peter's mother-in-law lying in bed with a fever and he was moved to action: 'When Jesus arrived at Peter's house, Peter's mother-in-law was sick in bed with a high fever. But when Jesus touched her hand, the fever left her. Then she got up and prepared a meal for him' (Matthew 8:14–15, NLT).

When Jesus heals Peter's mother-in-law, her first response is an act of hospitality. She prepares a meal for him out of gratitude for what he has done. Her hospitality is fuelled by love.

Having people round for a meal may have been something that, before having children, you did regularly, effortlessly and with enjoyment. In your new situation, hospitality may have become extra challenging. If you're the kind of person who likes to spend hours preparing the food and making your home ready for your guests, then things may have to change. If you like cooking, you may have to become an expert at doing things one-handed. There's also the question of how to organize hospitality around a baby's needs. On many occasions we've tried to get our daughter to bed at her usual time before the guests arrive, but she's woken up and we've spent most of the evening rushing up and down the stairs, trying to settle her between courses.

Peter's mother-in-law shows us what's really important about hospitality – that it is an act of service motivated by love. How can you enjoy being hospitable? How about hosting a lunch with your baby present, where everyone brings something to share? Or inviting someone from your antenatal group or a neighbour around for coffee and cake? How can hospitality be an enjoyable act of love this week?

Act and pray

Exercise hospitality this week to someone who would appreciate it. Try not to choose someone you know really well. Invite God to be part of the experience, asking him whom to invite and how he wants the time to work. Don't be too ambitious, and remember to plan beforehand how your baby will be included.

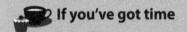 **If you've got time**

1. In Revelation 3:20 Jesus says, 'Here I am! I stand at the door and knock. If anyone hears my voice and opens the door, I will come in and eat with him, and he with me.'

   Imagine eating a meal with Jesus. What do you talk about? How does he make you feel? Have a conversation with him about whatever you want. Enjoy his company.

2. Read the quote from Yolanda below. Can you relate to it in some way? Read the story of Mary and Martha in Luke 10:38–42. Which character do you relate to more? What is Jesus saying to you?

3. Remember a time when you were invited to eat with someone and they made you feel really welcome. What was it about that occasion that you enjoyed so much? Ask God to help you grow in the gift of hospitality.

'Before, I would always mop the floor and tidy if people were coming round. I would cook a three-course meal from scratch. But when Mercy was born I decided I wasn't going to get stressed if people came over and the house wasn't perfect. That was really freeing. We still had people round quite a bit for dinner, as we still wanted to have a social life. I just didn't cook a three-course meal from scratch any more. I definitely didn't do a starter, and sometimes I had to let go of making a pudding and bought one instead. Cooking is a big thing for me, and I wanted people to think, "You're a really good cook", but it was just too tiring, so I did simple stuff and didn't worry about it. The point was that people were coming round to see us and hang out, not to have an amazing meal.'

Yolanda, mum to Mercy, two, and Solomon, five weeks

Related to this theme:
Month 11, Week 3: Mothers in the Bible: Rebekah

Month 6: Re-establishing Life Patterns

Week 4: What's your maths?

By Louie

> I will refresh the weary and satisfy the faint.
> (Jeremiah 31:25)

Will and I arrived home exhausted from the long drive back from Devon, where we had spent New Year. Having unpacked and got Skye to sleep, we collapsed on to the sofa, ready for a dose of mind-numbing TV. But we couldn't switch on the TV.

The following day, my laptop packed up. Then four inches of snow fell overnight. It was a start to the New Year that I would never have predicted: I was marooned at home with a young child, with every local baby-focused activity cancelled because of the weather. Without the usual technological crutches to entertain or distract, I was forced to think outside the box when it came to 'down time'. For the first time in months, I got out my sewing machine and completed a long-abandoned project.

I find it so easy to fill my evenings, and the times when my children sleep during the day, with housework, emails and TV. Those things that restore and refresh – which for me means getting my creative juices flowing or enjoying some exercise – are often left by the wayside.

Helen, mother of three adult children, shared with me how, as a new mum, she deeply valued time spent engaging in the things that revived her.

'When I had Gemma, my eldest child, I found that I just wasn't using my brain any more. I have always loved playing around with figures – I used to be a maths teacher. So I would get my textbooks out and do half an hour, or open an old exam paper and make sure I could still work through it. In the early days of motherhood, it was all nappies and talking to other mums about sleep patterns, and I found that hard. With the maths, I could get it correct and have a sense of achievement; it stimulated me.'

When there are things to do in the home, or pressing work deadlines, it can seem selfish or frivolous to spend time doing something purely for your own enjoyment. Perhaps the thought leaves you feeling guilty – you feel you should always be doing something useful or something that helps a loved one.

The verse above is part of God's promise to his people, the Israelites, that a time is coming when the weary will be refreshed (Isaiah 40:31). God cares about his children's exhaustion and weakness. So where a recreational activity revives our spirit and restores our verve for life, it can enable us to give more than we otherwise could. Ask God to bless your 'maths' this week, and refresh you through it.

 Act and pray

What's your maths? Perhaps you haven't recently thought about what revives you, let alone invested in it. Reflect on this now, and then carve out time this week to do it. Tell your spouse or a friend when you plan to do this, so they can help ensure that it happens. Invite God to be in this activity with you. He created you with passions and gifts: worship him through using them.

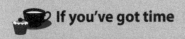 **If you've got time**

1. Meditate on Isaiah 40:31 as you enjoy a creative activity. Several versions of the Bible translate the first line of this verse as, 'But those who *wait* for the Lord's help find renewed strength' (NET Bible). Use this 'me time' to *wait* and *hope* in him, trusting him to renew your strength as nothing and no-one else can.

2. In *Gardening the Soul*, Sister Stan writes:

   'Ni h-é an t- éadaigh an fear (clothes do not make the man).' This old Irish saying tells us, in no uncertain terms, that the things we possess do not and will not define us, nor bring us peace and happiness. Some may still believe that abundant possessions bring happiness or that they are a sign of God's favour, but most of us know that when we are least reliant on material things we are happiest.[2]

The good things in our lives come from God, and there are times when these can be rightly enjoyed. But if you are relying on material things instead of God to restore you, ask him for forgiveness.

3. Finding a regular monthly or weekly time to do an activity that restores you can be a challenge. Pray about and commit to a regular time you could set aside for an activity you enjoy.

'When Mercy has a nap in the afternoon, I use that hour to do something I want to do – whether that's something creative, some sewing, watching TV or reading a magazine. There'll always be more work to do, so I've got to let go.'

Yolanda, mum to Mercy, two, and Solomon, five weeks

 Related to this theme:
Month 6, Week 2: Time for time out

Month 7: Exploring Your Baby's World

Week 1: The power of story

By Louie

Every evening after their bathtime, I snuggle up with my children and a few familiar storybooks and we read together before they go to sleep. I love that window of time with them. Childhood experts agree that reading to a baby is fantastic for their development, stimulating their senses and helping to develop their listening and memory skills.

We are all part of God's story. What part are we playing?

A few years ago, an American Christian author named Donald Miller wrote a best-selling memoir, *Blue Like Jazz*.[1] Not long afterwards he was approached by a production company which wanted to turn the book into a film. I recently read his latest work, *A Million Miles in a Thousand Years*,[2] which unravels how he and two film producers (Steve and Ben) wrote the story of his life for a movie. Along the way, Miller explores the metaphor of life as story. He writes:

> When Steve, Ben, and I wrote our characters into the screenplay, I felt the way I hope God feels as he writes the world, sitting over the planets and placing tiny people in tiny wombs. If I have a hope, it's that God sat over the dark nothing and wrote you and me, specifically, into the story, and put us in with the sunset and the rainstorm as though to say, *Enjoy your place in my story. The beauty of it means you matter, and you can create within it even as I have created you.*[3]

Before you were born, God wrote the story of your life into his divine meta-narrative. Your child will also play a part in the God-story. Your child has a special place in God's book of life, his plan for our world. Jeremiah 29:11 says, '"For I know the plans I have for you," declares the LORD, "plans to prosper you and not to harm you, plans to give you hope and a future".' Reflecting on this jolts me into prayerful action – I pray that each day my children will fulfil God's destiny for them, and that his purposes for their futures will come to be. Proverbs 19:21 says, 'Many are the plans in a man's heart, but it is the LORD's purpose that prevails.'

The story that you tell with your own life is the story you invite your child into. What kind of story do you want to tell as an individual, and as a family? Miller writes: 'We teach our children good or bad stories, what is worth living for and what is worth dying for, what is worth pursuing, and the dignity with which a character engages his own narrative.'[4]

 **Act and pray**

This week, read your baby a Bible story or some prayers from a children's prayer book. (See our Resources section on page 232 for ideas.) Here are some suggestions to help you:

- Ask God to speak to your child and touch them by his Spirit. Of course he/she won't yet fully understand a prayer or Bible story read aloud, but God does work in our children's hearts, even when they cannot communicate anything of this with us.

- Perhaps reading the Bible to your baby each day might become a 'trigger' for prayer, reminding you to pray that, as they grow up, they would see God through the Bible's stories and develop their own passion for his Word.

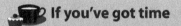 **If you've got time**

1. Write a short story in simple language about your life story so far, including how God has led you, and the things he has enabled you to do. Keep it somewhere safe and when your child is old enough, read it to them.

2. Literature and film offer us a range of stereotypical characters: the hero, the beautiful princess, the villain, the wizard, to name but a few. Reflect on the stereotype of 'mother' that culture depicts. What can you glean from it, both positively and negatively? To what extent do you feel pressure to live according to the stereotype? What character traits is God asking you to develop at the moment?

3. How does the following verse affect your sense of identity? What is God saying to you through it? 'For we are God's workmanship, created in Christ Jesus to do good works, which God prepared in advance for us to do' (Ephesians 2:10).

'One of the unanticipated joys of new motherhood was seeing that my son was a completely separate person, with his own desires and personality. As strange as it sounds, I wasn't prepared for that. I thought he'd be a combination of his father and me. It's been a tremendous joy to get to know this new little person in such an intimate way, right from the beginning of his life.'

Delana, mum to Tuck, fourteen months

 Related to this theme:
Month 5, Week 2: Getting to know your baby

Month 7: Exploring Your Baby's World

Week 2: A childlike faith

By Anna

> But Jesus called the children to him and said, 'Let the little children come to me, and do not hinder them, for the kingdom of God belongs to such as these. I tell you the truth, anyone who will not receive the kingdom of God like a little child will never enter it.'
> (Luke 18:16–17)

At seven months, Eliana was doing some serious vocal experimentation. It started well with lots of cute cooing and gurgling, eliciting appreciative smiles from old ladies at the supermarket. But then her favourite sound became a noisy, wet raspberry. Eliana blew raspberries when meeting new people and during the 'silent' prayers at church. This didn't go down too well. And neither did her next noise: a shrill, pterodactyl-style screech which my husband named her 'war cry'. Not only did the war cry intimidate other babies, but Eliana chose my husband's ordination at St Paul's Cathedral to practise it. From the dirty looks the lady in front gave me during the service, I think a war almost broke out!

One of the qualities that I love in children is their lack of inhibition, expressed through play, noise and open delight. Despite my embarrassment, the way Eliana 'plays' and experiments with her vocal chords, unhindered and freely expressing herself, unaware of social norms, is refreshing for me as an adult. This lack of inhibitions in babies is captivating, and I sometimes wonder whether this was one of the things in Jesus' mind when he drew his disciples' attention to the qualities of a child in the passage above.

The disciples had been looking, as many of us do, for status and position. Jesus' unexpected response is to highlight the importance of childlike characteristics in inheriting the kingdom of heaven. As well as the lack of inhibitions that many children exhibit, other childlike qualities are trust, dependence and humility.

In the early stages of weaning, I was amazed at how Eliana took whatever food I gave her. It was as if she knew that whatever came from me was good. She trusted me and was dependent on me to give her sustenance. Some babies take a while to get used to solids, but their trust is still the same. Do I have that same trust in, and dependence on, my heavenly Father?

I have mentioned a few characteristics of childlikeness, but there are many more. What aspect of childlike faith is God challenging you to grow in?

A starting point can be learning to 'play' and enjoy a childlike freedom rather than feeling hindered by social expectations. Playing with your baby is not just an expression of love, but a way in which you can learn from them. I sometimes feel silly playing games with Eliana and think I should be doing 'more important adult jobs', but God challenged me to have a 'playful faith' instead of taking myself too seriously: a faith that values exploring new things rather than being stuck in a rut, enjoying God's good gifts and expressing love openly.

I am also learning not to live under the expectation of how others think my daughter and I ought to behave. As we walk along and Eliana screeches happily, you may find me joining her with a loud singing voice! As we learn to be more childlike in our approach to God, to play, to trust and to delight in him, we will begin to understand what a good and loving Father he is.

 Act and pray

This week, follow your child's lead and learn what it means to be childlike. As you play with your baby, pray that God would make you uninhibited in your faith. As a symbol of this childlikeness, engage in physical play with your baby, such as bouncing on the bed or doing a crazy dance to your favourite music. Or try messy play, such as getting your hands mucky with your baby in mashed potato or porridge!

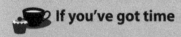 **If you've got time**

1. Reread Luke 18:16–17 slowly. Imagine that you are one of the children that Jesus is beckoning forward. What can you see, hear and smell? Ask Jesus to reveal himself to you and teach you more about childlike faith.

2. 'If you, then, though you are evil, know how to give good gifts to your children, how much more will your Father in heaven give good gifts to those who ask him!' (Matthew 7:11).

As you feed your child this week, giving them good gifts to sustain them, reflect on your own relationship with your heavenly Father. Are you dependent on him? What good things does God want to give you?

3. Forget your adult sensibilities and schedule in your own play time. Play can be boisterous, energetic, quiet, light-hearted or serious. Do something you really enjoy: get messy with paints, play a musical instrument, or perhaps read your favourite book.

'Even though my children are such monkeys sometimes, I love them ridiculously. It's brought me closer to God because I realize that God loves me infinitely more. Parenthood has taught me a lot about the father heart of God, and how he looks on me. There are lots of lessons I've learnt through how I've treated my children. For example, when they ask me for something that isn't good for them, like can they eat loads of chocolate, and I say "no", I realize that when I ask God for things he answers me as my parent.'

Susie, mum to Jed, four, and Lily, fourteen months

Related to this theme:
Month 1, Week 1: Our Creator God

Month 7: Exploring Your Baby's World

Week 3: Adventure or fear?

By Louie

She is bold and courageous. She is married, and she is a mother.

In Judges 4 and 5, we read the story of Deborah the prophetess, the only woman to lead the nation of Israel. Deborah was respected by her people and successfully maintained peace in Israel for the forty years that she was in power, leading her army to victory over Israel's enemy, Sisera.

Judges 5 is referred to as Deborah's song. Here, Deborah acknowledges that Israel has been through tough times, but that God has called her to bring her nation to victory and humbly to glorify him in the midst of hardship. She says:

O Lᴏʀᴅ, when you went out from Seir,
    when you marched from the land of Edom,
the earth shook, the heavens poured,
    the clouds poured down water.
The mountains quaked before the Lᴏʀᴅ, the One of Sinai,
    before the Lᴏʀᴅ, the God of Israel.

Village life in Israel ceased,
    ceased until I, Deborah, arose,
    arose a mother in Israel.

So may all your enemies perish, O Lᴏʀᴅ!
    But may they who love you be like the sun
    when it rises in its strength.
(Judges 5:4–5, 7, 31a)

Deborah trusts deeply in God, and obeys him in her particular situation as a prophetess and leader. Although her calling was unique, there is much we can learn from her courage and adventurous faith as she, in God's name, takes authority over fear (verses 7 and 31).

How courageous are you in your faith at the moment? In the midst of your family responsibilities, are you allowing God to challenge you out of your comfort zone and into a new level of trust in him? Or is your life full of worries and potential dangers for your child?

As a child starts to explore his or her surroundings, new opportunities for accidents present themselves. As parents, our natural instinct is to protect. While we do need to provide our child with a safe environment, he or she also needs freedom to discover their unfolding world. Simply doing this can mean trusting God in a bold new way ourselves, especially if the style of parenting we ourselves grew up with was a particularly anxious or fearful one.

Carole, mum to eight-month-old Billy, said, 'I am paranoid that something dreadful is going to happen to Billy as he explores the house. What I pray is, "God, give me the patience and understanding to let him grow, and be kind to us." I ask God to protect Billy, watch over him, and as he takes little steps, to cushion some of the bounces.'

Where is God calling you to step out in faith at the moment? Do you need to ask him to renew an adventurous spirit within you?

 Act and pray

Find a tape measure, and extend it to 10 cm. Imagine that every centimetre represents a year of your baby's life; so the next ten years are there before you. Pray prayers of protection for your child, and ask for God's will to be done in their life over those ten years. Put the tape measure on the floor, and extend it to around 80 cm. Walk along next to it, praying for your child's future.

If you've got time

1. In 2 Timothy 1:5, Paul extols Timothy's grandmother and mother as women of great faith, who have given Timothy a wonderful gift. Paul writes, 'I have been reminded of your sincere faith, which first lived in your grandmother Lois and in your mother Eunice and, I am persuaded, now lives in you also.' Is there a legacy of faith-filled mothers in your family? If so, thank God for them. Ask God to speak to you about how

you can model 'sincere faith' to your child, and pray that the generations to follow you will continue to pass on the gift of faith.

2. If you have started 'baby-proofing' your home, take a walk around it, and as you see cupboard locks, socket covers and stair gates, pray for an increase of God's presence. Ask him to bless your home as a place not only of security, but also of discovery and adventure.

3. Hebrews 11:4–12 reminds us of some of the Bible's great men and women of faith. Read these verses, perhaps looking up some of the stories they refer to. How are you challenged by them? Do something this week that requires an adventurous step of faith on your behalf – or a new, exciting activity for your baby.

'For me, having a baby was about the freedom of becoming a grown-up and making decisions for myself about my daughter. Up to that point I had still felt like my parents' child. God has freed me to be my own person and to make decisions. You have to figure out for yourself what's OK.'

Yolanda, mum to Mercy, two, and Solomon, five weeks

 Related to this theme:
Month 11, Week 2: Mothers in the Bible: Jochebed

Month 7: Exploring Your Baby's World

Week 4: Through your baby's eyes

By Anna

I was snatched abruptly from my activity mat, and before I knew what was going on, strapped tightly into my buggy. Mum put a sunhat on me, and then we went out into the glaring sunshine.

My eyes squeezed shut as the sun shone into them, and my body jolted as Mum pushed me over the gravelly pathway. I could smell something strange as we passed a man pushing a sharp-toothed metal machine which juddered across his lawn.

Then it got cooler, and as I looked up, there were tall brown sticks with green hats everywhere that seemed to be as high as the sky. The light coming through them made my arms all spotty.

Suddenly I heard a sharp 'woofing' noise, and a moving ball of hair, attached to a long piece of string, approached the buggy. It panted and licked my foot, and I thought how funny it looked.

This is a snippet from my seven-month-old daughter's journal (!) after I took her for a walk in the woods and she was turning her head from side to side, mouth slightly open, in an awestruck pose.

Have you ever thought about what the world looks like through your child's eyes? Babies can challenge us to relearn a sense of wonder at the world around us. We are forced to stop, listen, look and appreciate God's creation, whether it's a bird singing, the bobbly texture of a toy, or the intricate pattern on a rug. We literally become 'wonder-ful'!

David says in Psalm 8:

> O Lord, our Lord,
>   how majestic is your name in all the earth!
>
> You have set your glory
>   above the heavens.
> From the lips of children and infants
>   you have ordained praise
> because of your enemies,
>   to silence the foe and the avenger.
>
> When I consider your heavens,
>   the work of your fingers,
> the moon and the stars,
>   which you have set in place,

what is man that you are mindful of him,
  the son of man that you care for him?
  (Psalm 8:1–4)

David celebrates the glory and grace of God, seen in creation and in children, which then leads him to a place of wonder and reverence. One interpretation of verse 2 is that God's glory is displayed when children grasp and rejoice in the simple truths of God.[5] When babies demonstrate joy in the things they see, hear, touch, smell and taste, could this be their way of grasping and rejoicing in the simple goodness of God? How can we do the same?

One way is through being attentive. We can find traces of God's majesty in everyday things, such as the delicious rattling of a baby shaker, the sweet smell and plump softness of baby skin, and even the gloopy moistness of milk and baby rice!

Jesus was brilliant at seeing the kingdom in everything, using examples such as yeast (Luke 13:21) and coins (Luke 15:8–10) in his stories. Have we lost that childlike sense of awe at our Father's heavenly gifts? G. K. Chesterton said, 'Wonder will never be lacking in this world. What is lacking is wonderment.'[6] As we follow our child's lead and practise being attentive, let's pray for God's guidance so that we can be truly wonder-ful.

Act and pray

In Genesis 28:16b, Jacob says, 'Surely the LORD is in this place, and I was not aware of it.'

Practise attentiveness, using something small (perhaps your child's toy), and something vast (try looking at the sky). What do they teach you about God?

☕ If you've got time

1. Sit on the floor and observe your baby playing for five minutes. What are they experiencing through their senses? Pray that God would speak to you through your new perspective.

2. Genesis 1:31a says that 'God saw all that he had made, and it was very good'. Take your baby somewhere you consider beautiful. As you walk around, pray a simple prayer, such as: 'Lord, you are so good and your creation is so good. Thank you. Amen.'

3. There are things that prevent us from being attentive. Consider fasting for a time from something that distracts you. For example, fasting from TV or the car may help cultivate attentiveness – or fasting from sending text messages on your mobile phone could enable you to notice what's going on around you.

'I started to do things in new ways when I had Jamie. You spend a lot of time on your own with the baby. I used to chatter away to Jamie as we walked along and point things out as we went: "Look at the trees, Jamie" and "Listen to that wind blowing". It made me feel close to God and focused me on the wonder of my surroundings.'

Ruth, mum to Jamie, seven, and Finlay, five

Related to this theme:
Month 5, Week 1: Finding treasure

Month 8: Making Decisions

Week 1: Listening to God

By Anna

> But I have stilled and quietened my soul;
>> like a weaned child with its mother,
>> like a weaned child is my soul within me.
>
> (Psalm 131:2)

I was reluctant to wean my daughter. I had got into a routine of feeding her milk, and weaning meant entering into the unknown. I had heard of babies who threw food on the floor and spat out what they didn't like. It all sounded rather messy.

The psalm above talks about a fully weaned child who is no longer dependent on milk but has matured on to proper food. Jesus said, 'My food is to do the will of him who sent me and to finish his work' (John 4:34). God desires that we become mature in our relationship with him, feeding on him by listening to him, and obeying his will.

It can be easy to have a relationship with God that involves what I call 'shopping-list prayers'. We constantly ask God for the things we want, but never take time to listen to his agenda. In many ways, relying solely on these kinds of prayers is a bit like being forever dependent on milk and not moving on to solid food.

When I got pregnant, I had three months of feeling so incredibly tired and ill that all I could do was sleep. God started to strip away the frenetic activity in my life and teach me to listen to him as I anticipated motherhood. My prayers became less like shopping lists and more like a true relationship. I began to enjoy 'being' his child rather than constantly 'doing' things for him. To be still and quiet like a weaned child meant to stop wriggling around like a baby often does, and to feed on him in a new way.

This month we will be exploring some of the decisions you may be facing about the future. It is always easy to go to God with an agenda: 'God, help me with this' or 'God, give me guidance on that.' But God wants a mature relationship with his children, which is two-way. Are we prepared to enter into the more uncomfortable place of asking God 'what is on your heart?' and simply sit, like a weaned child, and listen?

This is a challenge with a baby. Anneke, mum to Rosie, fourteen months, found a way of doing this: 'I need half an hour of quiet each evening after Rosie goes to bed, when I switch off the TV or radio and just relax. Then God's peace comes. I give all my decisions to him, the big things and the small things. I can then receive from God. It's easier to listen to God and think things through this way rather than trying to make time in the day.'

If finding 'listening' space at home is impossible, you could go on a retreat while someone babysits, or meet up with a friend further on in their spiritual journey to listen to and learn from God together. Weaning *is* messy and uncomfortable, but also rewarding. As we feed on God by listening to him, we can be sure that we will see fruit growing in our lives: the reward of an intimate walk with Jesus.

Act and pray

'Very early in the morning, while it was still dark, Jesus got up, left the house and went off to a solitary place, where he prayed' (Mark 1:35).

Jesus made a habit of withdrawing from the crowds and praying to his Father. Find a minimum of five minutes on your own this week to sit and listen to God. Come to him with no agenda and simply ask, 'God, what is on your heart?'

If you've got time

1. 'He set himself to seek God in the days of Zechariah, who instructed him in the things of God; and as long as he sought (inquired of, yearned for) the Lord, God made him prosper' (2 Chronicles 26:5, Amplified Bible).

   King Uzziah's life depended on seeking God. Plan an extended period of quiet and stillness and ask God who he wants you to be and what he wants you to do.

2. What experience of solitude would you like to have two years from now? For example, you may want to go on an annual retreat away from home or incorporate a weekly prayer walk into your routine. Take steps towards your goal this week.

3. Try incorporating 'listening time' into part of your everyday routine, for example, every time you make a hot drink.

'I found Psalm 131 verse 2 really helpful to meditate on when I had Toby. To be calm and content like a weaned child is a challenge. I realized that I didn't always have to be doing the right thing, but instead I could sit and be peaceful with God, like the way my baby sat on my lap.'

Liz, mum to Toby, two

 Related to this theme:
Month 1, Week 4: Nourishing your baby

Month 8: Making Decisions

Week 2: To work or not to work?

By Louie

I breathed a huge sigh of relief and began to dry my tear-stained face. I had finally made the decision: I wasn't going back to work.

Unfortunately for my employer, I came to this conclusion the night before I was due back in the office, but I had been deliberating for months. There were so many factors to consider: I loved my job writing for a Christian magazine, and relished the thought of child-free time to develop my career. Financially, living off a clergy salary was a challenge, but God had always provided for us. I also wanted to prioritize my marriage, family and church life, which I knew meant not being in a permanent rush.

Whenever I tried to think and pray through these concerns, I got lost in a fog. One evening, I was driving and praying when it dawned on me: I was constantly evaluating my choices in the light of what others would think of me. If I decided to go back to work, would my family think I was putting my career before my child's needs? But if I gave up my job, would it mean an end to my career and financial security?

Paul writes in Galatians: 'Am I now trying to win the approval of men, or of God? Or am I trying to please men? If I were still trying to please men, I would not be a servant of Christ' (Galatians 1:10).

I needed to remember that verse again. Whether or not we mums work (in an official, paid capacity – all motherhood is hard work!), there will always be others making decisions that contrast with our own. Alison, mum of three, said, 'The hardest thing I have ever done is give up my career as a solicitor . . . Having kids has had a profound impact on me in that I have begun to understand how God values us for who we are, not what we do. You think you already know that, but until you give up your job and let yourself be stripped of all those things, you don't actually know it.'

I certainly wouldn't recommend myself as a model of how to go about the process of communicating with your employer at the end of your maternity leave! What matters is that eventually I came to a decision that I felt was right before God. I knew the road ahead wouldn't be an easy one, and it was a step of faith to wave goodbye to the familiar. But, finally, I felt his peace.

 **Act and pray**

If you are making a decision about whether or not to return to work, draw a picture representing yourself in the various possible circumstances you are considering, including significant elements affecting your choice, such as family, finances, church or your emotions. If you have already made a decision, draw yourself in the situation you will be moving into. Pray about your choice and how it works alongside your other priorities.

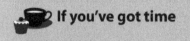 **If you've got time**

1. Reflect on the idea of 'your contribution'. Ask God what you uniquely bring to family life. Look up 1 Timothy 5:9–10 and Mark 9:36–37. What do these verses teach us about how Jesus values the raising of children?

2. In 2 Corinthians 12:9 God says, 'My grace is sufficient for you, for my power is made perfect in weakness.'

   Do you experience the sufficiency of God's grace in your life? Whether or not you are employed at the moment, pray about what it means for you to be without the status of having a job. Ask God to help you know him as sufficient, and to lay aside the need for labels in order to understand your identity.

3. Colossians 3:23–24 says, 'Whatever you do, work at it with all your heart, as working for the Lord, not for men, since you know that you will receive an inheritance from the Lord as a reward. It is the Lord Christ you are serving.' Use these verses to ask God to help you work as if you are working for him.

'As a working mum, I felt a tension that I don't think the stay-at-home mums felt. I was caught between two worlds and trying to juggle work and motherhood. A lot of mums feel guilty about this, and sometimes your worlds collide. But I think that women are very adept at moving seamlessly between the two worlds. You have to ask yourself: "How can I make this work?"'

Ruth, mum to Jamie, seven, and Finlay, five

 Related to this theme:
Month 8, Week 4: The Proverbs 31 mum

Month 8: Making Decisions

Week 3: Trusting God with your money

By Anna

Prima Baby magazine ran a survey revealing that pregnancy and the first six months of a baby's life cost mothers an average of £10,000.[1] Whatever our financial circumstances, money can be a source of worry. Will I be able to provide everything my child needs? Should I pay for private nursery care? Will my part-time salary be enough?

When making choices about work, childcare and the future, it's easy to let fear rather than trust in God form the basis of our decisions. If we don't have much money, we worry that our child will go without essentials. If we have enjoyed a good salary we may feel vulnerable if we sacrifice it, or pressurized to maintain a certain lifestyle.

When I was pregnant, my husband and I were both reliant on a student grant. When I found out that we would be receiving less grant money than we had anticipated, I broke down, sobbing. Didn't God care about our baby? My answer came in the post the next day, when a huge box of washable nappies worth over £300 and two lovely baby slings arrived from an old friend – what a provision! God was demonstrating that he would provide everything our baby needed, but not in the way we expected.

Jesus taught his disciples to pray: 'Give us today our daily bread' (Matthew 6:11).

Praying for our daily bread is not just about praying for enough to eat, but praying for God's ongoing provision. Kenneth Bailey translates this verse as follows: 'Deliver us, O Lord, from the fear of not having enough to eat. Give us bread for today and with it give us confidence that tomorrow we will have enough.'[2] Do we trust that our Father's supply for our family will never run out?

We should also note above the word 'our' rather than 'my'. What we have does not belong to us as individuals – it is for sharing. When we pray for 'our daily bread', we must be open to being generous to others with what we are given. Generosity flows from a heart that is thankful and content. Paul says:

> I know what it is to be in need, and I know what it is to have plenty. I have learned the secret of being content in any and every situation, whether well fed or hungry, whether living in plenty or in want.
> (Philippians 4:12)

The passage doesn't say we will always have plenty. The important question is: have we learned the secret of being content in any and every situation?

Sometimes we might envy our friend's top-of-the-range buggy, or resent the mum who can afford to stay at home while we have to go back to work. Perhaps we are tempted to use our money to impress others.

God wants us to cultivate thankfulness and contentedness. He wants to enable us to hold lightly to what we possess. Instead of envying others, thank God for his gifts. Instead of resenting other mums, ask God to help you love them. Instead of using your money to gain status, do something generous with it.

Bring to God any fear you have regarding money. Allow him to bring you freedom to enjoy the money he has given you, and to be content whatever your circumstances.

 Act and pray

Spend time examining your attitude towards money before God. Decide to make one positive change this week. Is God asking you to:

- Give something away?

- Be a better steward?

- Be content whatever your circumstances?

- Make a tough decision based on trust?

Tell a friend what you have decided to do, and ask them to keep you accountable to your agreement.

If you've got time

1. Those of us who pray the prayer above in Matthew 6:11 affirm that all we have is a gift from God. Think about a decision you have to make about money. How might this perspective help you to make your decision?

2. Throughout the day, deliberately cultivate thankfulness by thanking God, even for the small things.

3. Giving generously can be fun, and breaks the power that money often holds over us. Give something away this week – perhaps write a cheque for a friend or leave a bar of chocolate on someone's doorstep with a note.

'I was on maternity leave, and Ruby was three months old. My old company was being taken over, which meant I would not have a job to go back to and my maternity pay would stop . . . But I was not ready to start looking for another job with Ruby so young. It was a really dark time, and I couldn't understand God's plan. But after eight weeks we received two sums of money from two couples! What they didn't realize was that it was the exact amount that we needed to cover my lost maternity pay up to the time I had intended to go back to work. It was perfect!'

Suewan, mum to Ruby, two

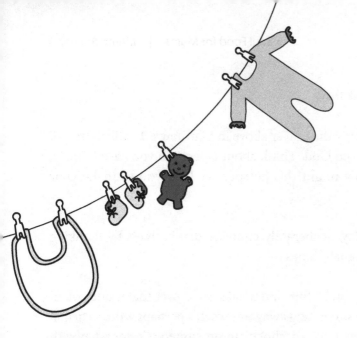

Month 8: Making Decisions

Week 4: The Proverbs 31 mum

By Louie

A wife of noble character who can find?
   She is worth far more than rubies.

She selects wool and flax
   and works with eager hands.

She considers a field and buys it;
   out of her earnings she plants a vineyard.
(Proverbs 31:10, 13, 16)

Proverbs 31:10–31 gives us an insight into the world of an Old Testament wife and mum. This mum enjoys her work – toiling eagerly (verse 13), and getting up while it is still dark to provide food for her family and servants (verse 15). She is a shrewd businesswoman and ensures her earnings provide a return (verse 16). But verse 10 reminds us that, whatever our working status, of greatest value to God and our family – worth even more than any material thing – is that we cultivate a 'noble character'.

God wants us to develop a noble character, both in our vocation as mum and in any other vocation we may have outside the home. Is God calling you to develop a noble character in the workplace?

Jane, mum of two, shared the story of her return to work when her first child, Peter, was nine months old: 'From when I was a teenager, I knew I wanted to be a doctor. I felt that that was what God wanted me to be, so I decided to return to work. I prayed about childcare and about finding a new job, as well as what hours to work. When I went back, I realized that my priorities had changed, and being a mum came first, which meant not working overtime but leaving earlier to pick Peter up from nursery. I get a lot of satisfaction from my work, and it felt good not to be changing nappies all the time. In my work I felt like I was making a real difference. It was also good to have predictable hours, set coffee breaks and adult company.'

If, like Jane, you are considering returning to work, you may be making several other choices too, including deciding on childcare for your baby. Will you trust God to provide for both your child's needs and your own, in the transition back to work?

Rhoda, a mum of four, was anxious about finding the right childminder for her daughter Elinor and asked God to make it clear whom to choose.

She was shocked when the first childminder she visited had left her own three-year-old playing on the street – clearly this wasn't the right person! The second childminder asked if she could smoke during Rhoda's visit – not the right person either! But the third childminder had a son of a similar age to Elinor, which meant that all the activities she put out for him were appropriate for Elinor too. Rhoda's search had ended: God had provided, and had made the decision simple and obvious.

God wants to be included in your decision-making regarding potential employment and childcare. However you feel about the possibility of going back to work, trust that God is able and willing to equip and guide you, your child and your family on the anticipated and unanticipated journey ahead.

 Act and pray

Look up Proverbs 31:10–31 in your Bible. What other values do you see in the Proverbs 31 mum? Think about:

- The way she relates to her husband (verses 11–12, 28–29)

- Her attitude towards her work, both domestic and business-related (verses 13, 17–18, 27)

- Her response to those in need (verse 20)

- The foundation on which her success is built (verses 26, 30)

Pray about the values you have identified. How can you develop them in your own life?

If you've got time

1. If you are currently considering what sort of childcare to choose, seek out the wisdom of more experienced mums from church and ask them to share their experiences with you. How did God play a part in their decision-making?

2. Becoming a mum or adding a child to your family may have changed your career-related goals. Ask God how he wants you to approach your working life at the moment, and in the future.

3. If you are back at work, use the pauses during your working day to look at the clock and reflect on what your child might be doing at that particular time. Pray for your child in these moments, whether he or she might be napping, eating or playing with other children.

'I found the transition from mum-life to landing back in my office very emotional and strange. It was like stepping back into my old life but as a completely different person. Gradually it became more normal, and as Elsa settled in childcare, I began to enjoy teaching again and the opportunity to grow that side of my life once more.'

Veronique, mum to Elsa, two

Related to this theme:
Month 8, Week 2: To work or not to work?

Profile of a mum

Focus: Adoption

We adopted Leo from my sister when he was eight months old. I also have a stepdaughter, Carly, who was five when I became her mum, so I've never been through the baby stage before.

Carly's mum died when Carly was two, and she has always found it difficult to accept me as a mum. I think she thought I was stealing her dad when we got married. She would treat me as an older sister.

There have been some real challenges since adopting Leo. I've found that all of a sudden I have to slow down. I can't do everything I used to do. I've not been getting much sleep or doing any housework lately. It was my birthday recently and I just fell asleep at 8 pm!

There have been some real joys too. I've been able to take Leo and the dog outside, put a rug on the ground, sit in the sun and look at the trees, and just have time to enjoy being a mum. I've been able to point things out to Leo and teach him about the world God has made. That's been brilliant.

Adopting Leo has also helped my relationship with my stepdaughter. She loves Leo, and I think that now there are two of them together she accepts me more as a mum. She sees me caring for Leo and treats me like an adult now.

I had been feeling distant from God for a while before we adopted Leo, as we had been through a family crisis. My sister had four other children as well as Leo and was not coping. I wanted to adopt them all. On top of that, when Leo was born he had a severe medical condition, but miraculously the surgery he had at birth went well. Through this experience I have seen that God is so faithful. He understands if we can't pray sometimes. He understands when we are just trying to do the right thing.

When you adopt a child you are very aware that your child is a gift from God. They belong to him. Adoption has helped me to understand my relationship with God better. God adopts us into his family when we become Christians. He takes us in and nurtures us. We are his. In the same way that Leo now chooses to come to me, to look for me and to seek me out, I know God wants me to choose to come to him, look for him and seek him out.

Trisha, mum to Leo, ten months, and stepdaughter Carly, eight

Month 9: Looking Outside Your World

Week 1: Servant-heartedness

By Louie

When Skye was four months old, 'The Baby Way' was launched at our church, St Peter's, West Harrow. This was a new ministry, designed to serve and reach out to the local community, particularly parents and carers of babies under one year old. The Baby Way is a drop-in baby-weighing clinic, with hot drinks and home-made cakes for parents, as well as excellent medical advice and a chance for the building of vital new friendships.

For the previous few years, my friend Sam, mother of three children under four, had been praying about a vision she felt God had given her for our church to set up something innovative like this. Finally her God-dream was coming to life! We were both excited because our church building hosts a Christian-run doctors' surgery, and this was a wonderful opportunity for church volunteers to work together with medical staff to show the love of God in practical ways.

If I hadn't been a mum of a young baby, I would probably never have caught Sam's vision. As parents of young children, we can think that our opportunities to serve God and build his kingdom must now be dramatically limited. In fact, entering a new season can bring with it a window of fresh opportunity for God.

Jesus teaches us: 'If any of you wants to serve me, then follow me. Then you'll be where I am, ready to serve at a moment's notice. The Father will honor and reward anyone who serves me' (John 12:26, *The Message*).

Looking beyond our immediate world to the needs of others calls for a prayerful, creative approach, especially when we are parenting young children. We have our children's needs to consider, as well as our own desire to obey Jesus' call to serve him. Helping at The Baby Way has sometimes presented problems for me as a mum, particularly during those tricky months when babies become clingy and yell their protestations at being put down for even a moment.

Despite the challenges, as our children – however young they are – watch us serving God in our daily lives, they see an example to follow as they grow. I have also found the message of the verse above, that God honours and rewards anyone who serves him, to be true. God has provided a wonderful team to run The Baby Way with Sam and me. We have had fun and become closer friends through our involvement. Being there is also good for my children, who enjoy playing with the toys and other children, eating the delicious home-baked cakes and getting cuddles from the volunteers! As I serve God, I trust that he will honour what I'm choosing to do by making it a positive experience for my children too.

It may be that the primary place where you are called to serve God in this season is within your family. Or is God challenging you to step out in faith and start serving outside your home? Is it time to return to helping at church in some of the ways you did before parenthood? Perhaps, in this new season of your life, God is calling you to serve him in a new way.

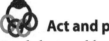 **Act and pray**

Read the parable of the talents in Matthew 25:14–30, and ask God to speak to you about how you are using your talents at the moment. What talents – skills, abilities, resources or passions – has God given you? Write these down as a list, if this helps. How might God want you to bless others with these talents? Contact your church leader and talk to him or her about the ways in which you could serve at church at the moment.

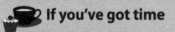 **If you've got time**

1. Look up Zechariah 4:6, Psalm 127:1 and Proverbs 11:25. What do these verses tell you about the approach God wants you to take as you serve?

2. Liaising with your church leader, organize a prayer walk focusing on the needs of your local area. This activity doesn't need to be limited to mums only!

3. Try typing 'serving' into your mobile phone or internet search engine. If your phone does predictive texting, then you may find that the word 'resting' comes up as an alternative option. Reflect on the idea that serving God can be restorative.

'At house group this morning, we spent five minutes discussing how one of the group who had just had a baby was doing. So I said, "Well, I'll just go and phone her now, because then we'll know how she is." And she said, "I'm struggling; please pray for me." Later we started talking about how nice it would be to have biscuits after the church service because then people would stay and chat more, rather than scuttling off home without chatting. So I suggested that we all take a packet of biscuits on Sunday. How hard is it to say, "Let's just do it"?'

Ruth, mum to Isla, five, Carys, two, and Keira, six months

 Related to this theme:
Month 11, Week 4: The mother of James and John

Month 9: Looking Outside Your World

Week 2: Loving and learning from those who are different

By Anna

As mixed-heritage parents, my husband and I are trying to ensure that in the future our daughter will understand her ethnic identity. We have compiled a book which includes aspects of the Indian, Malaysian, Caribbean, African and English parts of her history, and we are also learning about parenting in other countries. Sometimes it's easy to be prejudiced about how people from other cultures or walks of life bring up their children, but as we build relationships with those we see as different, we learn about ourselves, other people and God.

Encountering people who differ from us culturally, socially or because of their circumstances presents opportunities for growth and change. I was recently challenged by a friend who brought her children up in a rural setting – I've always lived in towns and cities – and gave them the freedom to grow chilli plants, rear chickens and drive tractors!

We all have something to learn from others and something to offer. We may be scared of people who are different from us but, as we get to know them, we discover that we are actually surprisingly similar! We also begin to appreciate rather than judge their differences as we understand their world. This is the foundation of loving others.

The ability to love truly comes from God: the God who lived a life of love on earth alongside those who were 'different' or on the margins. We love others because of who God is and the way he has poured his love into our lives:

> Dear friends, let us love one another, for love comes from God. Everyone who loves has been born of God and knows God.
> (1 John 4:7)

This love pushes us out of our comfort zones. It means seeing people as Jesus sees them, rather than as they superficially appear. It may mean talking to that mum who seems to have an alternative way of parenting. It may include inviting the mum with difficult foster kids over for a coffee.

Anneke, mum to Rosie, fourteen months, shares: 'One day I prayed, "Lord, please show me who to be with today." I went along to our local toddler group and ended up talking to a single mum with four children, and was able to encourage her as well as learn from her. I also met another woman who was looking after her sister's baby as the baby's mum was a prostitute. I was bowled over by this opportunity to meet people whom I wouldn't normally meet. I think it was a case of not having an agenda and wanting to be used by God.'

Do you want truly to love and learn from those who are different from you, and for your child to do the same? Perhaps God is already beginning to give you a deeper empathy for particular people in your circle of influence. Whom can you start to love, serve and learn from today?

 Act and pray

A friend shared an acrostic with me which he calls 'the pathway to love'. Use the principles below this week when you meet someone whom you see as different from you. Think of one way in which you could begin to teach your child one of these principles as they grow.

L isten – Listen to God about the person, to your own responses to them, and to what they say

O bserve – See them as God does

V ulnerability – Share and give something of yourself

E mpathy – Identify with the person without feeling that you need to be identical to them

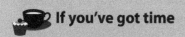 **If you've got time**

1. Think of a mum in a different situation from you. Pray for the challenges she may be facing.

2. Do you know a mum from another country? Ask her to tell you about motherhood and child-rearing in her home country, and pray that through her God would teach you something new.

3. In Sweden there is a tradition of the father being the first person to dress the new baby. This helps dads to bond with their child. Thank God for the diversity he has created in his world, demonstrated in other cultures. Confess to him any prejudices you have.

'I was told to put my daughter in her cot for a nap during the day, but in many countries babies are practically strapped to their mothers in cloth slings for five years! Their whole identity is literally "wrapped up" in the identity of their mum. In the Jewish culture weaning was traditionally done at five years old, which enabled real bonding between mother and child. I breastfed my daughter until she was one. Sometimes that was awkward, like when I was breastfeeding in church and people could hear sucking sounds coming from under my shawl. In India, where I grew up, this was normal.'

Karen, mum to Louise, eighteen, and Sam, sixteen

 Related to this theme:
Month 10, Week 3: Walking with the wise

Month 9: Looking Outside Your World

Week 3: Mum and evangelist

By Louie

> . . . Thanks be to God, who always leads us in triumphal procession in Christ and through us spreads everywhere the fragrance of the knowledge of him. For we are to God the aroma of Christ among those who are being saved and those who are perishing. To the one we are the smell of death; to the other, the fragrance of life. And who is equal to such a task?
> (2 Corinthians 2:14–16)

As I write this, I am pregnant with my second baby. One of the many strange things about pregnancy is an incredibly heightened sense of smell. I notice the delicate fragrance of a blossoming flower as I walk through my garden, or feel my stomach churn while simply putting some rubbish into my kitchen bin.

In verse 15 above, we read that, in God's view, we are 'the aroma of Christ' to those around us. Whether they are Christians and are 'being saved', or do not yet know God and so 'are perishing', we bring something of Jesus' love and grace – perhaps unseen and unspoken, but yet powerfully present – to each person we make contact with. You carry the 'fragrance of the knowledge of him' about your person (verse 14). How does that make you feel? Excited? Privileged? Unworthy?

'Babies are incredible for evangelism!' This was what Rhoda, mum of four, discovered. She continued: 'People stop and talk to you when you have a baby with you – you are a lot less threatening. One of the first people I ever helped become a Christian was a pregnant woman I met on the bus when I was expecting Elinor. We had something in common, and she used to come round to our house. When her daughter was born, she and her husband turned to us for support. They became Christians, having come from a background of atheism.'

Paul tells us that some people will react well to the aroma we carry as Christians, recognizing on us 'the fragrance of life'. Others will acknowledge God in us as 'the smell of death' (verse 16). So we need courage to wear this bold perfume, as well as the intuition of the Holy Spirit, to discern how others are reacting. Rhoda shared with me: 'When people commented on how beautiful my daughter was, I would say, "Yes, God has really blessed us." Then I would gauge their response, to see if I could take the conversation further. Sometimes I would say to friends, "I was asking advice from another mother at church . . . Do you go to church?"'

These were Rhoda's ways of openly showing others that God (and church) were a central part of her life. Let's remember that, without God's grace, none of us is 'equal to such a task' (verse 16), and yet, as Paul also wrote, 'I can do everything through him who gives me strength' (Philippians 4:13).

 **Act and pray**

This week, allow your sense of smell to inspire you to pray. Notice the variety of smells around your home, neighbourhood (and, if relevant, your workplace). Each time you notice a smell, recall these words from 2 Corinthians 2:15a: 'For we are to God the aroma of Christ . . . ' Prayerfully repeat this phrase several times now, asking God to help you remember it this week.

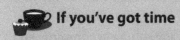 **If you've got time**

1. Think about your typical week: the places you go to and the groups of people you see regularly. How could you serve God within one of these settings? Think of one person on the edge of one of those groups – perhaps a new work colleague or mum at the toddlers' group. Pray this week for God to reveal himself to that person. Show them friendship next time you see them.

2. Reflect on the following verse:

> How beautiful on the mountains
>> are the feet of those who bring good news,
> who proclaim peace,
>> who bring good tidings,
>> who proclaim salvation,

who say to Zion,
  'Your God reigns!'
(Isaiah 52:7)

Use this verse to inspire prayer. You could:

- Thank God for your feet, and the different people and places they take you to. Pray for your child's feet, that they too would be beautiful to God as the feet of a person who shares him with others.
- Look at the verbs used in the verse above. What is God asking you to bring, to proclaim and to say?

3. Look up 2 Corinthians 5:11–21. What could you do this week to be an ambassador for Christ?

'I try to have one day a week when I don't have an agenda. That way I can be available to people. I pray, "God, let me make a difference." Sometimes you feel your prayer isn't being answered, but the truth is that, wherever you go, you are shining God's light and spreading his fragrance. Sometimes you can't see anything, but you have to trust and be ready to be used.'

Anneke, mum to Rosie, fourteen months, and seven months pregnant

Related to this theme:
Month 5, Week 4: God working in your child's life

Month 9: Looking Outside Your World

Week 4: Seeing the bigger picture

By Anna

Think about the last time you read the newspaper or watched the news. What stories moved you? What stories made you angry? Most likely, these stories connected with your values or passions, which have been planted in you by God and can be used to help you pray for concerns in the world.

I have always found it difficult to pray for global issues as they seem faceless, distant and disconnected from my own life. When I became a mum, my world became even more focused on the here and now. I also didn't know what to pray for, as I felt I didn't know enough about the subjects. Maybe you have started working again and are just about managing motherhood and holding down a job. One mum said to me,

'Once I had a baby, I couldn't switch on the news. I found it too distressing!' *All* these things can prevent us from praying about the wider concerns of God's heart.

The good news is that the Holy Spirit helps us to pray, interceding for us:

> In the same way, the Spirit helps us in our weakness. We do not know what we ought to pray for, but the Spirit himself intercedes for us with groans that words cannot express.
> (Romans 8:26)

A good starting point for prayer is beginning with what we know about God's character. God is a God of justice and mercy who cares about the world he has made.

> . . . And what does the LORD require of you?
> To act justly and to love mercy
>   and to walk humbly with your God.
> (Micah 6:8)

How can we live lives of justice as busy mums?

First, we can start where we're at, rather than feel guilty about what we're not praying about. I like to pray for a charity I used to work with that helps prostitutes to gain freedom from a life of exploitation and addiction. I also have a friend who manages a hostel for homeless girls, who is 'acting justly and loving mercy'.

Secondly, you may find it easier to pray for situations that you can relate to or for people in similar circumstances to yours. Hazel, mum to Zephan, eight months, shares what happened when she was struggling as a new mum: 'God awoke in me a new compassion for mothers across the world. Sometimes I just couldn't bear the thought that there were new mothers who were going through exactly the same thing but without access to medical care and sufficient food and water . . . Now I am determined to find small ways of helping new mothers, whether it's the new mum up the street or by supporting charities overseas.'

The Micah verse above calls us to 'act', 'love' and 'walk'. As you start to pray for others, the Holy Spirit may prompt you to take action and become the answer to your own prayers. As we pray, we don't know how God is going to lead us to respond. But we can be encouraged that our prayers and actions do make a difference and will be part of God's work of justice in the world.

 Act and pray

Imagine what the world will be like in eighteen years' time when your baby is an adult. What kind of world would you like your child to grow up in? Listen to what God is laying on your heart as you reflect on this, and then pray. How is he prompting you to take action now?

If you've got time

1. If you find it difficult to pray for world affairs, then be honest with God and thank him for his Spirit. Ask him to help you see things as he sees them. Use the following verse to help you pray: 'I will give you a new heart and put a new spirit in you; I will remove from you your heart of stone and give you a heart of flesh' (Ezekiel 36:26).

2. When you watch, read or listen to the news, pray that God would awaken his compassion in you for an issue, a people group or a situation. Use this compassion to pray.

3. Look up the words 'justice' and 'mercy' in a dictionary or, if you have one, a Bible dictionary. What insight is God giving you into these words, and how will this knowledge transform you this week? Pray that your child would eventually exhibit justice and mercy in their life.

'Hearing about tragedies in the news made me question my faith like never before, as I became more empathetic about the pain of losing a child. Every time I have been through periods of doubt in life, it has ultimately led to a deepening of my faith because it drives me to pray and push into God, and also gives me more empathy when in relationship with people who are hurting.'

Hazel, mum to Zephan, eight months

 Related to this theme:
Month 12, Week 3: Being part of a global family

Month 10: Learning to Parent

Week 1: Loving your child

By Anna

According to John Lennon, 'Love is all you need', but learning to express that love as a parent is not always straightforward. What does it mean to love a child who flatly refuses to feed? When your child screams uncontrollably every time you leave the house, how do you demonstrate love? How could God help you love a baby who cries all night?

For some mums, a strong sense of love for their child doesn't come at the moment of giving birth. Love isn't necessarily a fuzzy feeling, but is about a choice and an act of the will. Love is a process. You can choose to love your child, and pray that your feelings follow that choice.

God is love. Our role model for how to love our children is found in Jesus, whose love was extravagant, sacrificial and unconditional:

> Be imitators of God, therefore, as dearly loved children and live a life of love, just as Christ loved us and gave himself up for us as a fragrant offering and sacrifice to God.
> (Ephesians 5:1–2)

The first verse above reminds us that we are dearly loved children. Knowing we are loved helps us to live the life of love we are called to as parents. When our children seem difficult to love, we can ask God to give us his love for them, which is immeasurably deeper, stronger and more patient than our own!

The love God has for you as his child is infinite and unconditional. Not only has he forgiven you for every wrong thing you have ever done or thought, but he continues to demonstrate this love by caring for you, answering your prayers, transforming you and delighting in you. Do you know this love at the core of your being? This is the love that will ground you in your parenting and transform your own life as a child of God.

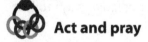 **Act and pray**

> And this is my prayer: that your love may abound more and more in knowledge and depth of insight, so that you may be able to discern what is best and may be pure and blameless until the day of Christ.
> (Philippians 1:9–10)

Write these verses on a piece of paper and carry it round in your handbag or wallet. When you have a spare moment, perhaps while waiting at the surgery or in the supermarket, look at the verses and use them to pray for yourself, your spouse and other mums you know.

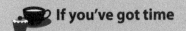 **If you've got time**

1. Find your favourite photo of your baby and sit and look at it for a couple of minutes. How does it feel to be looking at your child? Reflect on your love for your baby. If you find it difficult to love your baby, then ask God to give you his love. Ask God to show you how much he loves you. If you are overwhelmed with love for your baby, thank God that his love for you is even more overwhelming.

2. If you have not had the experience of unconditional love from your own parents, you may find it hard to love your own child unconditionally. If you feel this is a problem for you, then talk and pray with your minister or a counsellor.

3. How can you demonstrate your love for your child in new ways? On three Post-it® notes, dream up three practical or creative ways to love your child this week.

'I have learned a lot through my love for Ruby. I recently read that a child can never be loved too much. I don't want to spoil Ruby so I won't give in to her every demand, but I do tell her every day how beautiful she is and how much we love her. I pray with her every bedtime and let her know that God loves her too.'

Suewan, mum to Ruby, two

 Related to this theme:
Month 2, Week 1: Baby first

Month 10: Learning to Parent

Week 2: Laying foundations for parenting

By Louie

> I will show you what he is like who comes to me and hears my words and puts them into practice. He is like a man building a house, who dug down deep and laid the foundation on rock. When a flood came, the torrent struck that house but could not shake it, because it was well built.
> (Luke 6:47–48)

What sort of foundations are you putting down as you parent a young family? In the parable above, Jesus teaches us to build wisely – to make him the foundation of everything in our lives. He is to be the root of our confidence, our life decisions and our day-to-day choices.

But the one who hears my words and does not put them into practice is like a man who built a house on the ground without a foundation. The moment the torrent struck that house, it collapsed and its destruction was complete. (Luke 6:49)

After Jesus has taught about the man who 'comes to me and hears my words and puts them into practice' (verse 47), he describes the opposite response. The second man in the parable has heard Jesus' words, but chooses not to implement them (verse 48). The home built without Christ as its foundation cannot withstand the storm, and crumbles to nothing.

What differentiates the approaches of these two men is encapsulated in a word that we don't often like to mention: obedience. Usually I find that the choice God calls me to make is not the one I naturally want to go for. But this parable reminds us that living in obedience to God is the wisest way to live, and enables us to build families that can weather the toughest of life's storms.

In my first year of motherhood, I found myself increasingly thinking about what it meant to parent a child. How could we raise a happy, confident person with her own relationship with Jesus? Suddenly my own – and my husband's – life choices and values were thrown into the spotlight afresh, because I knew a little person was already watching and learning from our every move. Would our daughter truly see us living out what we professed, that Jesus was our first love? Patrick Kavanaugh says, 'We cannot expect our children to be any more dedicated to Christ than we are ourselves.'[1]

The sixteenth-century Spanish nun Saint Teresa of Avila noticed her parents' godliness at the age of just six or seven. 'It was a help to me that

I never saw my parents inclined to anything but virtue, and many virtues they had. My father was most charitable to the poor, and most compassionate to the sick, and also to his servants; so much that he could never be persuaded to keep slaves . . . My mother too was a woman of many virtues . . . '[2]

When your child, or children, are adults, and reflect back on their childhood, what godly characteristics do you hope they will remember seeing in you? In the next chapter of this book (Month 11), we explore some of the characteristics of mothers in the Bible.

Act and pray

Talk and pray with your spouse this week about your approach to parenting. How are you building a firm foundation for your family? If you are parenting alone, discuss this and pray with a close friend, family member or godparent.

If you've got time

1. Learn more about what it means to parent as a Christian. You might like to buy a book on the topic or attend a Christian parenting course. For ideas, see our Resources section, on page 228.

2. Do you have the support you need to parent effectively? Who can you seek advice from, or pray with, about the difficult aspects of parenting? Could you join – or start – a group with other parents at a similar life stage? Pray for God's wisdom and provision.

3. Use the following poem to affirm to Jesus that you want him as your foundation:

> O Lord, seek us, O Lord, find us
> In thy patient care;
> By thy love before, behind us,
> Round us everywhere;
> Lest the god of this world blind us,
> Lest he speak us fair,
> Lest he forge a chain to bind us,
> Lest he bait a snare.
> Turn not from us, call to mind us,
> Find, embrace us, bear;
> By thy love before, behind us,
> Round us, everywhere.[3]

'You don't acquire the skills to be a parent overnight. You learn through trial and error and by making your own decisions. There's no perfect way to parent. The challenge is the level of guilt you feel. You get messages thrown at you all the time from magazines and other parents – I was in the park the other day, and one mum said to another, "Isn't your baby cold?" As mums, we need to say to each other, "You're doing fine" more often.'

Ruth, mum to Jamie, seven, and Finlay, five

Related to this theme:
Month 12, Week 4: Looking to the future

Month 10: Learning to Parent

Week 3: Walking with the wise

By Anna

> He who walks with the wise grows wise,
>> but a companion of fools suffers harm.
> (Proverbs 13:20)

Sometimes it feels as if I have a huge red 'Learner' plate stuck to my forehead saying 'Look, everyone – I don't know what I'm doing!' It isn't just first-time mums who feel this. More experienced mums can feel desperate when their tried-and-tested parenting methods don't work with baby number two or three.

After ten months of parenting, I thought I was a pretty confident mum, but there were still times when I had to call the health visitor, phone a friend or trawl dubious parenting internet sites with my questions. What helped was having more experienced mums around me from whom I could learn.

One couple with older children had always done a job-share and spent an equal amount of time looking after their two children. They consistently involved their children in decisions such as schooling or moving house. We deliberately sought to learn from their example.

I met up with this wise, older mum once Eliana was born, to pray and talk about parenthood and life. By spending time with her I was seeking to 'walk with the wise', as the proverb above says, and hopefully grow a bit wiser as a parent in the process.

Many mums gain wisdom on parenting from their own mothers or family, especially if the latter live close by. In Old Testament times a family unit would have lived in a compound of two or three houses representing extended families of about a dozen members and up to four generations.[4] Imagine living with and learning from your great-grandma! Many communities around the world still live like this today.

Each of us comes from generations of family that provide us with a rich heritage of mothering from which to draw inspiration, although for some that heritage has not always been ideal. If you have a good relationship with your family or they live nearby, you have an opportunity to 'walk with the wise' in this way. Why not ask your mother or grandmother about her parenting, and pray that God would teach you through her insights?

If your family is more scattered around the country, as it is in our case, experienced friends can teach you just as much. When our daughter was born, a friend came to help me navigate the tricky world of new motherhood and kept me sane in the process!

What kinds of qualities should we look for in someone we learn from? Proverbs 18:15 outlines the qualities of a wise person: a permanent learner who is continually alert for ways in which they can grow, listen to others and gain new understanding:

> Wise men and women are always learning, always listening for fresh insights. (Proverbs 18:15, *The Message*)

This week, ask God to provide you with a 'mum mentor' from whom you can learn and with whom you can meet regularly to pray about parenthood, someone who will listen to you and inspire you. It may be that God eventually calls you in turn to mentor others in the same way, passing on the wisdom you have learned.

Act and pray

Next time you put your shoes on, pray about the person whose footsteps you want to follow in. Invite them to be your 'mum mentor'. If finding a mum mentor is tricky, then allow yourself to be mentored by one of the inspiring mums whose books are listed on page 228.

If you've got time

1. 'In everyone's life, at some time, our inner fire goes out. It is then burst into flame by an encounter with another human being. We need to be

thankful for those people who rekindle the human spirit.' (Albert Schweitzer, theologian)[5]

Dig out some old photo albums, letters or emails. Who are the people who over your lifetime have rekindled your spirit? Reflect on their contribution to your life so far, and thank God for them.

2. We all have wisdom to pass on to others, no matter how inexperienced we feel. Is God calling you to encourage a brand new mum? If so, begin to pray for her needs and take steps towards befriending her.

3. Being a 'disciple' of Jesus means committing to learning from his teaching, following his example in mission and being empowered by the Holy Spirit. Reflect on how Jesus succeeded in turning his disciples from ordinary men and women into people who transformed the world with the gospel (Mark 4:1–20; Luke 10:1–24; John 20:19–23).

'I went to a seminar at a Christian conference on parenting pre-schoolers. The speaker had picked four families with "well-rounded" children and asked them what the key to their parenting was. The common thread was that each of the families said they had brilliant kids and liked spending time with them: they actually liked their children and enjoyed them! That is something I hope and pray will be the key to my parenting too.'

Claire, mum to Josiah, four months

 Related to this theme:
Month 9, Week 2: Loving and learning from those who are different

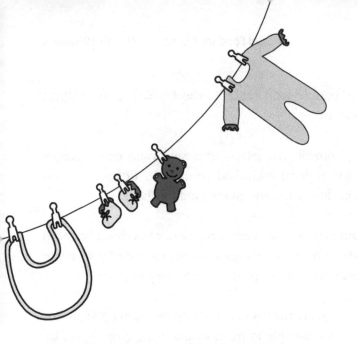

Month 10: Learning to Parent

Week 4: Reflecting on your own childhood

By Louie

On one of my parents' bookshelves is a dusty, overflowing box file, stuffed with memorabilia from my childhood. In among the photos, poems, stories and drawings, I found a school exercise book from when I was six years old. Dated 'Wednsday 21st Sepembr' was my version of the story of Noah's ark:

> Long ago God said that Noah must billd a arc and take one of eche anamil. And then go in yourself. And it will rain and rain because people fite. And then you send out a duve and he did and the duve came back with leevs and Noah bumped into land.

Looking back, it seems amazing that I knew this part of the Bible so well at such a young age. My knowledge of that story – and my wobbly ability to draw and write – was all thanks to those who took the time to teach me.

The teacher who will have the greatest impact and influence on your child (or children) is you! In the book of Proverbs we read: 'Train a child in the way he should go, and when he is old he will not turn from it' (Proverbs 22:6). At the moment, what are you deliberately taking the time to teach your child? You may be helping them to crawl or walk, or teaching them to feed themselves. By your living, breathing example, you will also be teaching them about more complex concepts, such as love, peace and respect. What might you be inadvertently teaching your child, both positively and negatively?

Since becoming a parent, you may have found yourself thinking more than ever before about your own childhood, and what your parents taught you about life. You may also find that you respond to your own parents in new ways because now you share in their experience of having a child (or several). Alison, mum of three, said of when she became a mum: 'I became a lot more forgiving of my own parents. Now I appreciate them a lot more. When it comes to my own children, I know that they will only know how much I love them when they have their own children.'

Take time this week to reflect on your own upbringing, thinking and praying about what good things you learned from your parents, and what things you do not want to emulate.

Act and pray

Who have been the most influential teachers in your life? Make a list, including not only childhood schoolteachers, but also family members, friends or church leaders. Now single out one or two of them. What characteristics made each one a good teacher? What could you replicate from them as you teach your child? Thank God for the people on your list, and pray about your role as teacher to your child, bringing God any fears you might have about assuming this responsibility.

☕ If you've got time

1. What decisions or challenges are you facing as a parent at the moment? This week, talk and pray about these things with your spouse, or, if you are parenting alone, with a close friend or family member. Reflect on how your own parents' choices or example in the same areas may be affecting your respective approaches.

2. Dig out an old family photo album, and use the images to help you thank God for your parents. Focus on praising him for the good things they taught you and gave you as you grew up.

3. Susannah Wesley, mother of the influential hymn-writers John and Charles Wesley, took her role as teacher to her children very seriously. Even though she never preached a sermon or wrote a book, she has been called the 'Mother of Methodism'. Find out a bit more about this influential mother this week and ask God to inspire you from her life.

'It's amazing what you replicate from when you were parented. Although you don't remember being a baby, you end up doing what your mum did with you. I say to myself, "That's just what my mum used to do!" I guess you internalize things that were done for you. A lot of things are learned behaviour and not in the genes. If you've seen someone picking up a crying baby, then that's what you know to do, but those who haven't been modelled unconditional love sometimes don't know how to give it.'

Ruth, mum to Jamie, seven, and Finlay, five

Related to this theme:
Month 4, Week 3: A new season with your parents

Month 11: Growing in Character and Confidence

Week 1: Mothers in the Bible: Hannah

By Louie

It's hard to change your character once you are an adult, but it's not hard to help form the character of a young child.

This wisdom from another mum prompted me to consider: how can I expect to help form the character of my child effectively unless I regularly ask God to reshape my own character?

This month we focus on the defining character traits of four biblical mothers. As you read, ask God what he wants to change in you, so that you might become a more effective role model to your child, able to help form their character, under God's guidance.

We begin with a look at the story of Hannah becoming a mother for the first time.

> In bitterness of soul Hannah wept much and prayed to the LORD. And she made a vow, saying, 'O LORD Almighty, if you will only look upon your servant's misery and remember me, and not forget your servant but give her a son, then I will give him to the LORD for all the days of his life, and no razor will ever be used on his head.'
> (1 Samuel 1:10–11)

Hannah experienced the deep pain of being infertile (1 Samuel 1:5). To make matters worse, her husband's other wife, Peninnah, had many children and frequently taunted Hannah about her inability to conceive (1 Samuel 1:6). It is from this place of torment and desperation that Hannah cries out to God, pleading with him for a baby (verses 10–11). Hannah perseveres in prayer. Her persistent prayerfulness is a quality she brings with her into new motherhood.

You may have struggled to conceive as Hannah did. The authors of *Just the Two of Us: Help and Strength in the Struggle to Conceive*, write:

> Infertility can bring such disillusionment and disappointment that people can lose sight of who God is and what he is doing in their lives. This might be through thinking that a God who allows such pain cannot love them or through a dullness that causes them over time to stop going to church, meeting with other Christian friends, reading the Bible and praying.

The authors go on to quote from a woman named Amy who was facing infertility: 'Where is God in all of this pain? He is right beside me – I have found it hard to feel that He is there at times but I have learnt that it is not wise to always believe my feelings. Instead, I trust that He is the same faithful and loving God who doesn't change.'[1]

Perhaps like Hannah you once prayed fervently for a child, but now prayer doesn't seem as urgent. But Hannah isn't a quitter when it comes to prayer. She pours out her soul to God, even in the midst of 'great anguish and grief'.

When God does answer Hannah's prayer, she doesn't forget to act on the vow she made to dedicate her son's life to him (verse 11). She says, 'I prayed for this child, and the LORD has granted me what I asked of him. So now I give him to the LORD. For his whole life he will be given over to the LORD' (1 Samuel 1:27–28).

Act and pray

Reread the story of Hannah becoming a mum in 1 Samuel 1:1–28. What words would you use to describe Hannah's prayer life? What can you do this week to keep promises you have made before God, or to others? Have you dedicated your child back to God, who gave him or her to you in the first place?

If you've got time

1. What is God calling you to pray persistently about? It may be just one thing, but if several issues spring to mind, make a list in your journal. Pray about these things now.

2. Spend time thinking about your family prayer life. What would start to teach your children to pray? Patrick Kavanaugh suggests praying the Lord's Prayer together or praying 'around the circle' one at a time.[2]

3. Do you know couples struggling with infertility? Pray for them now. Ask God how, as a parent, you can be sensitive and loving towards them, gently including them in your own family life.

'I view prayer as my way to commit my dreams, desires and concerns for each of my children to my heavenly Father. My husband and I pray for our children together once a week. We both try to read the Bible and pray daily for and with each of them and we often have a corporate family worship time on a Sunday evening. What inspires me to persist in prayer is seeing faith grow in each of my girls – even my youngest, who is three.'

Rosie, mum to Hannah, seven, Abigail, five, and Rebekah, three

Month 11: Growing in Character and Confidence

Week 2: Mothers in the Bible: Jochebed

By Anna

'Now drop your baby.' The words from the swimming teacher shot terror through me and my response was to grip on to Eliana more tightly. I was being encouraged to allow my daughter to swim underwater by herself for the first time. Although I wanted her to become confident in water, I was nervous and didn't want to let her go. Despite my reluctance, I gently eased my grasp on Eliana's body for a few seconds and let her feel the water around her. To my delight, she began kicking and eventually she was making moves towards independent swimming.

There will come a time when we all have to let go of our children's hands, as we leave them with a babysitter and then relinquish them into the capable hands of their first teacher. As the years go on, we may see them taking another person's hand in marriage, holding their own child's hands, and then holding our hands again, steadying us in our old age! As we learn to let go now, we are taking steps towards trusting that God is our child's ultimate carer and that he uses other people to care for them too.

Moses' mother, Jochebed (we are told her name in Exodus 6:20), must have been afraid to let her baby go. She hid him in a papyrus basket among the reeds along the bank of the Nile, because the authorities at the time had made it the law to kill all Hebrew baby boys, and she understandably wanted to spare her child's life. She did what she could by sending her daughter to watch the baby.

God provides for baby Moses miraculously:

> Then Pharaoh's daughter went down to the Nile to bathe, and her attendants were walking along the river bank. She saw the basket among the reeds and sent her slave girl to get it. She opened it and saw the baby. He was crying, and she felt sorry for him. 'This is one of the Hebrew babies,' she said.
>
> Then his sister asked Pharaoh's daughter, 'Shall I go and get one of the Hebrew women to nurse the baby for you?'
>
> 'Yes, go,' she answered. And the girl went and got the baby's mother. Pharaoh's daughter said to her, 'Take this baby and nurse him for me, and I will pay you.' So the woman took the baby and nursed him. When the child grew older, she took him to Pharaoh's daughter and he became her son. She named him Moses, saying, 'I drew him out of the water.'
>
> (Exodus 2:5–10)

Jochebed lets go of her baby and entrusts him to God. God graciously honours her and gives Moses back to her in her role as nurse. She even gets paid for the childcare! Moses receives the blessing not just of his mother's care but also of the powerful influences of his sister and Pharaoh's daughter, the last of which sets the scene for his extraordinary calling. Moses is no ordinary child. He grows up as a man of faith, eventually leading God's people out of slavery in Egypt. This mother's decision was part of God's divine plan of salvation.

Leaving our children in the care of trustworthy people allows God to build our faith muscles and to use other people to give them what we cannot give them ourselves. The story of Jochebed is a powerful reminder that God has the resources and the compassion to look after our babies. Our children are gifts from God, and who better to entrust them to but him?

 Act and pray

Think of one situation where you struggle to 'let go' of your child, either physically or emotionally. When you next find yourself in that situation, pray a simple prayer of trust: 'Lord, I entrust my child to you.'

If you've got time

1. On a piece of paper or in a journal, finish the following sentence: 'Entrusting my child to God means . . . '

2. Slowly reread the story of Moses' mum in Exodus 2:1–10, and imagine you are experiencing her emotions at every twist and turn. Prayerfully ask God to speak to you in the process.

3. Spend time this week talking and praying with your spouse or a close friend about the people you trust to look after your baby. How can those people be part of God's provision for your child?

'At this stage it's about learning to let go, about trusting someone else to look after Billy when I am not there. And knowing that, when I am not there, Jesus is always with him.'

Carole, mum to Billy, eight months

Related to this theme:
Month 7, Week 3: Adventure or fear?

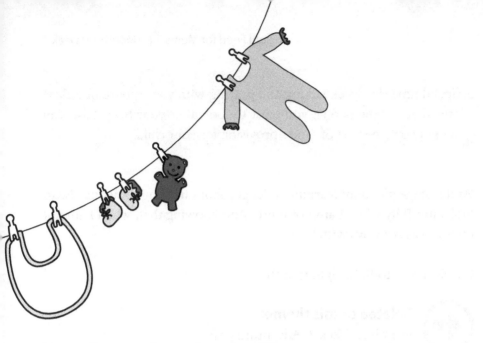

Month 11: Growing in Character and Confidence

Week 3: Mothers in the Bible: Rebekah

By Louie

> Before he had finished praying, Rebekah came out with her jar on her shoulder
> . . . She went down to the spring, filled her jar and came up again.
>
> The servant hurried to meet her and said, 'Please give me a little water from
> your jar.'
>
> 'Drink, my lord,' she said . . . After she had given him a drink, she said, 'I'll
> draw water for your camels too . . . '
>
> (Genesis 24:15–19)

Genesis 24 tells an unusual story of matchmaking and marriage. It is the account of how Abraham found a wife for his son Isaac, in a culture where arranged marriage was the norm.

In this passage Abraham sends his servant on a mission to find a suitable wife for his son Isaac. The servant arrives at his destination, heads for the town's spring for a drink after his long journey, and asks God to help him identify the right sort of woman for Isaac. He says to God, 'May it be that when I say to a girl, "Please let down your jar that I may have a drink," and she says, "Drink, and I'll water your camels too" – let her be the one that you have chosen for your servant Isaac' (Genesis 24:14). Even before the servant has finished his prayer, a beautiful girl appears, heading for the spring in order to fill her jar with water.

When the servant asks Rebekah for a drink, she shows a quality that he must have been hoping to identify in a potential wife for Isaac: kindness. Rebekah has the courage and generosity of spirit to take time to give a stranger a drink from her water jar (verse 18). But she doesn't stop there – she offers to get water for his camels too. Here is a woman with a servant heart who is willing to go out of her way to help, expecting nothing back. Perhaps Jesus had this story in mind when he taught in the Sermon on the Mount:

'If someone forces you to go one mile, go with him two miles. Give to the one who asks you, and do not turn away from the one who wants to borrow from you.
(Matthew 5:41–42)

Rebekah is unaware that she is an answer to another's prayer. But the servant sees that she is God's provision, lavishes expensive jewellery upon her, and offers her Isaac's hand in marriage, which she accepts.

In this story we see God richly rewarding a woman who chooses to put others before herself. Rebekah and Isaac have a happy marriage, and she is blessed with twin sons.

What part does kindness play in your marriage and family life? Are you willing to show kindness outside your 'inner circle' of family and friends, even to strangers? Where your kindness goes unnoticed in this world, God takes delight in it, rejoicing over your obedience to him and blessing you in ways of which you may be unaware.

 ## Act and pray

> Therefore, as God's chosen people, holy and dearly loved, clothe yourselves with compassion, kindness, humility, gentleness and patience. Bear with each other and forgive whatever grievances you may have against one another. Forgive as the Lord forgave you.
>
> (Colossians 3:12–13)

Think about one act of kindness you could do this week for a friend, neighbour or family member: something that is manageable in your circumstances, but which also requires servant-heartedness. Pray about your idea, asking God to help you clothe yourself with kindness.

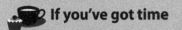 ## If you've got time

1. '. . . God's kindness leads you towards repentance' (Romans 2:4).

Reflect once again on the cross, and God's kindness shown to you through Christ's sacrifice for you. Is there anything that he is leading you to repent of today? Read Titus 3:4–7.

2. Look up the Sermon on the Mount (Matthew 5 – 7), and in particular Jesus' teaching within it on some of the principles brought to light in the story we have looked at in this devotion. How are you challenged by Jesus' instructions to love your enemies in Matthew 5:43–47?

3. Isaac clearly trusts the decisions his father makes on his behalf, accepting the wife Abraham has chosen for him. What qualities do you need to develop in order to teach your child/children to trust you? What is it about God that enables you to trust him?

'I sometimes sit and wonder, "What if . . . " What would happen if, every time I met another Christian, before we parted I said, "Shall we pray?" and we did just that? What would they do? What would God do? What would happen if, every time someone came to my house, I asked them, "Is there anything you need?", and they told me, and, if I had it, I gave it to them?'

Ruth, mum to Isla, five, Carys, two, and Keira, six months

Related to this theme:
Month 6, Week 3: A hospitable home

Month 11: Growing in Character and Confidence

Week 4: Mothers in the Bible: The mother of James and John

By Anna

> Then the mother of Zebedee's sons came to Jesus with her sons and, kneeling down, asked a favour of him.
>
> 'What is it you want?' he asked.
>
> She said, 'Grant that one of these two sons of mine may sit at your right and the other at your left in your kingdom.'
>
> (Matthew 20:20–21)

No-one likes a pushy parent. James and John, the sons of Zebedee, had a mum who certainly belonged in this category. Fancy asking for your sons to sit at the two most prestigious places in God's kingdom – his right and left hand! The disciples present were understandably outraged at her audacity.

Can you relate to this mother's plea? She wants the best for her children, and to ensure they get the place of honour. As a woman, her own status would have depended on that of her male relatives, so her pushiness could have been an attempt to gain status for herself as well.

Maybe she wanted the prestige of her sons being associated with a well-known rabbi. Then she could say to her friends, 'You'll never guess what my boys are doing now . . . They're with the great rabbi, Jesus. Some say he's the Messiah, you know . . . '

Jesus uses the situation to teach the disciples what servanthood is actually about:

> . . . Instead, whoever wants to become great among you must be your servant, and whoever wants to be first must be your slave – just as the Son of Man did not come to be served, but to serve, and to give his life as a ransom for many. (Matthew 20:26–28)

God's kingdom values are different from the values of this world. Radical discipleship means servanthood, sacrifice and humility rather than selfish ambition and competition. Desiring the best for our children is natural, but Jesus is clear that God's way doesn't involve elbowing past others. In God's kingdom the first will be last and the last will be first (Mark 9:35).

This is a challenge to us as mums. The radio and TV presenter Kirsty Young has criticized the 'modern disease' of pushy parents who try to shape their children into 'baby Einsteins'. She said that parents were 'preoccupied with children as an "extension of their own success"'.[3] Are we guilty of filling our weeks with limitless 'improvement' activities for our children which are actually more about us than them? Do we use our children to fuel our own self-esteem?

Paul says:

> Do nothing out of selfish ambition or vain conceit, but in humility consider others better than yourselves. Each of you should look not only to your own interests, but also to the interests of others.
> (Philippians 2:3–4)

It can be hard to look to the interests of others when we have our own feelings of personal unfulfilment. If we accept God's love for us, then we begin to grow in contentment and in the ability to model servant-hood and humility. This is the best advertisement for Jesus that we can give our children, and will show them what being a disciple of Jesus is all about.

Act and pray

When you are next in a situation where you are tempted to choose the quickest queue (e.g. at the supermarket), against your instinct, choose the longest one! Remind yourself of Jesus' words: 'If anyone wants to be first, he must be the very last, and the servant of all' (Mark 9:35). Pray that God would help you understand what radical discipleship means.

If you've got time

1. Ask five friends what they think 'humility' means. Contrast their

responses with 'humility' in the following passages (Titus 3:1–2; James 3:13; 1 Peter 5:5). Are there any similarities?

2. Philippians 2:5–11 is a beautiful description of the humility of Christ. Read this passage using the ancient monastic art of *lectio divina* (Latin for 'divine reading'), a way of praying with Scripture that involves studying, pondering, listening to and contemplating the Bible's words to bring us closer to Christ.[4]

3. Use the following prayer in a time of confession:

> Save me Lord, from the distraction
> Of trying to impress others,
> And from the dangers of having done so.
> Help me to enjoy praise for work well done,
> And then to pass it on to you.
> Teach me to learn from criticism,
> And give me wisdom
> Not to put myself at the centre of the universe.[5]

'I was more impatient with my first child and not at ease with myself. I expected too much of him. I felt guilty about that . . . Having children teaches you to be more humble about people and their frailty. You realize how fragile life is and what is important.'

Alison, mum to Ieuan, twelve, Jenny, ten, and Anwen, seven

Related to this theme:
Month 9, Week 1: Servant-heartedness

Month 12: Celebrating God's Faithfulness

Week 1: Reflecting on the past year

By Anna

Congratulations! You have reached the final month of the first year of your baby's life. You are probably experiencing a mixture of emotions. The journey may have had its challenges, dry patches and tough decisions, but no doubt it has also included elation, unanticipated joys and answered prayers.

As you look back over the past year, you may be able to discern God's faithfulness in the way he has watched over you and your baby, taught you about himself and encouraged you as a mother. The psalmist declares:

Not to us, O LORD, not to us
    but to your name be the glory,
    because of your love and faithfulness.
(Psalm 115:1)

For the Israelites, Yahweh's love and faithfulness were demonstrated in the covenant relationship. This acted as a reminder to them of God's unswerving commitment to them. Looking back and remembering is an important motif running through the Bible. Many of the Jewish feasts and festivals were celebratory reminders of God's goodness.

I have kept a journal since the age of eleven. Looking back and reminding myself of answered prayers and God's faithfulness fuels me for the next leg of the journey. We don't know what will happen next week, next month or next year, but we do know that God will remain faithful. His faithfulness to me also encourages me in my faithfulness to him and others. How can I walk more intimately with Jesus next year and how can I bless the people he has put in my sphere of influence?

If this year has been a difficult one, then looking back may be painful. Perhaps you can't see God's hand at work. For now, you may need to cling to God in the darkness, trusting in him despite the circumstances and knowing that you can find refuge under his wings. The psalmist says:

He will cover you with his feathers,
    and under his wings you will find refuge;
    his faithfulness will be your shield and rampart.
(Psalm 91:4)

God's care combines the warm protectiveness of a parent bird with the hard, unyielding strength of armour.[1] Knowing and experiencing this helps us to feel secure in him, just as our children are secure in us.

This security is the grounding for us as we move into the second year of our child's life. There may be challenges ahead, but God's faithfulness will not continue just in our lives but also in the lives of our children, and their children, and their children's children!

> For the LORD is good and his love endures for ever;
>> his faithfulness continues through all generations.
> (Psalm 100:5)

As we reflect on our baby's first year, which may be our first ever year of motherhood, let's remember the enduring love of our God that spans the generations and pray that we will remain faithful in our parenting, relationships and commitment to Christ.

Act and pray

Draw a simple timeline of the year, charting the highs and lows. What have you learned about God, yourself and others? What one thing has demonstrated God's faithfulness to you? The following categories may help:

- Your relationship with your child
- Your relationship with your friends and family
- God's provision
- Key Scripture
- Your prayer life
- New opportunities
- Funny stories

If you've got time

1. Look back at each month's devotionals and remind yourself of your journey and answers to your prayers. If you have kept a journal, look back at what you have written. Record the prayers God has answered.

2. Make or buy yourself a congratulations card. Display it somewhere as a reminder of God's faithfulness to you. If you know any other mums with a toddler approaching a year old, send them a card too.

3. The Lord's Supper is all about remembering: remembering what Christ did on the cross. Arrange to have your own simple meal with your spouse, a close friend or a group of friends, and celebrate together.

'Having children stopped me from being a control freak. My children had opinions of their own. I was no longer in control of my life. I now know what patience is and am much less selfish. I am a different person because of my children. Life is not all about me: I am part of a little community. If you are a control freak, the best thing to do is have three kids. Then you're outnumbered.'

Alison, mum to Ieuan, twelve, Jenny, ten, and Anwen, seven

Related to this theme:
Month 6, Week 1: Taking stock

Month 12: Celebrating God's Faithfulness

Week 2: Let's celebrate

By Louie

We recently celebrated Skye's first birthday, and I have just been reliving the memories with a glance at my photos of the day. Each one shows a hive of activity – toddlers chasing bubbles with cake-covered hands, mums happily buried in piles of toys and mess. Hardly an inch of kitchen floor can be seen through the mass of coloured plastic balls – we had to put the ball pond in the house as it was raining outside. It was a simple, joyful, active morning – just right for a first birthday party.

Reflecting on the day helps to remind me of what that party was about – not only offering hospitality to my daughter's little friends and their parents, but also celebrating her, the passing of the first year of her life, and the achievement of reaching the end of year one of motherhood.

This month you may be thinking about celebrating your child's first birthday. When children a little older than your one-year-old celebrate, they do it in style. It usually involves noise, dancing and singing. Watching children party reminds me of how reserved I can be as an adult. I wish I didn't have so many inhibitions, and could more often express freely with my body the way I'm feeling.

Zephaniah 3:17 says that God rejoices over you:

> The LORD your God is with you,
>   he is mighty to save.
> He will take great delight in you,
>   he will quiet you with his love,
>   he will rejoice over you with singing.
> (Zephaniah 3:17)

In Zephaniah 3, the prophet talks about the Day of the Lord, which had previously been described as a day of judgment and despair. It is now shown to be a day of joy and fearlessness because of God's presence with his people, and the heroic acts he has done for them.

We don't often think of God as a God of celebration: indeed, our culture often associates him with rules and regulations, depicting him as a killjoy. But the verse above shows the opposite to be true. Here God responds to us as an uninhibited, rejoicing parent, taking great delight in his children. To rejoice is to choose to be 'in joy' regardless of the circumstances. In this verse God reacts to us in joy, both by stilling us in the presence of his love and by singing over us.

You may not be feeling full of joy at the moment, especially if your child is ill or you are struggling with acute tiredness. Maybe choosing to celebrate this month will start with prayerful acknowledgment of the difficulties you face, alongside thankfulness for the blessings.

How can you begin to express celebration freely? David's life included many hardships as well as blessings, yet he 'danced before the LORD with all his might' (2 Samuel 6:14), and, after God saved the Israelites by parting the Red Sea, Miriam '. . . took a tambourine in her hand, and all the women followed her, with tambourines and dancing. Miriam sang to them: "Sing to the LORD, for he is highly exalted . . . "' (Exodus 15:20–21).

 Act and pray

Look up Moses' and Miriam's song in Exodus 15:1–21, and use this to help you to praise and rejoice. Make an active choice to be 'in joy' today, whatever is going on. Ask God to free you from your inhibitions as you celebrate both him, and your child becoming a year old.

If you've got time

1. God instructed the Israelite people to celebrate Passover each year, to remember how he saved them from destruction and plague. Exodus 12:14 says:

   This is a day you are to commemorate; for the generations to come you shall celebrate it as a festival to the LORD – a lasting ordinance.

Commemorating this event became central to Jewish history and culture. As you think about the future of your family life, what events do you hope to celebrate annually, and why? How could you creatively teach your child/children about God through each celebration? Discuss your ideas with your spouse or another close family member.

2. Look up Luke 15, where you will find three short parables of people or things that were lost, but are now found. What does each parable teach you? What does God rejoice about? How would you feel if you were the parent in the third parable, and how does this relate to God's response to you?

3. Practise worshipping without bodily inhibitions by taking time to praise and pray to God in different positions at home this week. Try:

- standing and praising, arms outstretched
- kneeling and thanking God for his provision
- lying prostrate in God's presence

'One of my favourite parables is the story of the Prodigal Son. Maybe it's because I just love parties! I love it when the dad throws a party for his long-lost child. It says to me that it is in God's nature to celebrate us, no matter what we've done or how we feel. I hope I can model this to my daughter as she grows up.'

Anna, mum to Eliana, seven months

 Related to this theme:
Month 4, Week 1: Investing in your marriage

Month 12: Celebrating God's Faithfulness

Week 3: Being part of a global family

By Anna

> Speak up for those who cannot speak for themselves,
>> for the rights of all who are destitute.
> Speak up and judge fairly;
>> defend the rights of the poor and needy.
> (Proverbs 31: 8–9)

The baby boy, as yet unnamed, was sleeping contentedly on his proud mother's breast. A few hours earlier I had witnessed his birth by Caesarean section at Kabala Hospital in northern Sierra Leone, as part of my work with international children's charity UNICEF. If this mum had given birth to her 10lb baby at home, without the doctor's help, which is common in

Sierra Leone, she and the baby would probably have died. In most Western hospitals, having a Caesarean section is nothing out of the ordinary, but in Sierra Leone it meant that both mother's and baby's lives were saved, though the hospital had no electricity and only two doctors for nearly 300,000 people. That day I witnessed a miracle.

Even in the twenty-first century, having a child remains one of the biggest health risks for women worldwide. To put things into perspective, one thousand women die every day from complications in pregnancy or child-birth, often because they cannot get much-needed medical help.[2] Having been through a year (or perhaps more) of motherhood, can you imagine having no access to a GP's surgery or vaccinations for your baby, or not being able to Google 'baby sleep solutions'?

This month we have been looking at celebrating God's faithfulness. How might we express that faithfulness in our love for others? The verse above calls us to speak up for those who are in need and cannot change their own circumstances. Many mums living in poverty cannot demand their basic rights, or the rights of their children to good health and a safe environment to grow up in. We have an opportunity to act prayerfully on behalf of mothers and children worldwide.

The following is an extract from my journal during Eliana's first week, written while still in hospital:

> Totally exhausted and in pain. Can barely walk down the corridor to the loo. Have been pulling the cord for pain relief from the midwife incessantly. But am glowing with pride. I've joined the worldwide club of global motherhood. Images in my drug-induced mind of the women I've met in Africa who've given birth in ridiculously difficult circumstances – no pain relief, no midwives

saying 'Push now!', no bottled water to gulp between puffs of gas and air. Mums really are amazing.

You may have recently spent time celebrating your child's first birthday. What could you do as a prayerful and practical response to God for blessing and protecting you and your child this year? When your toddler grows up, they will be encouraged to know that their life has inspired generosity towards another parent or child.

 Act and pray

Use your child's new life to bring someone else new life. To mark your child's first year, support a charity that helps women and/or children. For a list of charities that support women and children, go to the Resources section on page 231.

If you've got time

1. Suppose a brother or sister is without clothes and daily food. If one of you says to him, 'Go, I wish you well; keep warm and well fed,' but does nothing about his physical needs, what good is it? In the same way, faith by itself, if it is not accompanied by action, is dead.
    (James 2:15–17)

    What have you learned this year about putting your faith into action? Is God opening up new avenues for you as you enter your toddler's second year?

2. Angela Ashwin in *Patterns Not Padlocks* says, 'When we feel inadequate and ground down by the demands of parenthood in our own lives, we

are sharing, to some degree, the experience of millions of parents who struggle to bring up their children against all kinds of odds. So we can offer our own difficulties in an act of intercession for parents worldwide.[3]

Whatever struggles you have faced this year as a parent, use them to intercede for parents all over the world.

3. Throughout the Bible there are several commands to take care of widows, orphans and the fatherless (Exodus 22:22; Zechariah 7:10; Malachi 3:5). How might this apply to you as a twenty-first-century mum?

'As a newborn, our son spent a number of weeks in intensive care. Living in one of the most culturally diverse cities in the world, I quickly found myself relating to and empathizing with the other mothers around me. Our relationships transcended culture, language and religion. Through experiencing the love I had for my son, I was able to understand something of the universal heart-cry of all mothers.'

Sally, mum to Samuel, two, and Arabella, six months

Related to this theme:
Month 9, Week 4: Seeing the bigger picture

Month 12: Celebrating God's Faithfulness

Week 4: Looking to the future

By Louie

> In the course of one's life, one sows seeds. These seeds develop in the souls of other men and affect their destiny, and the fruit that is born of these seeds truly belongs not only to those who bear it but also to those who sow.[4]

During this past year, you have been sowing the seeds of love into the life of your new child. As you look ahead to their second year and beyond, you will continue to sow richly into their future.

The theme of planting seeds, and seeing them grow to fruition, runs throughout the New Testament. I love Jesus' image of the kingdom of heaven, as expressed in Matthew's Gospel:

The kingdom of heaven is like a mustard seed, which a man took and planted in his field. Though it is the smallest of all your seeds, yet when it grows, it is the largest of garden plants and becomes a tree, so that the birds of the air come and perch in its branches.
(Matthew 13:31–32)

This verse tells us that, as followers of God, we are part of the largest, most exciting and life-filled kingdom ever created. We have exponential potential within it. And this is the incredible spiritual place into which you are bringing your child, or children! From an apparently insignificant baby named Jesus of Nazareth came the mighty kingdom of heaven, and so too can God use a person like you or me, and a baby like yours or mine, to bring about his immense kingdom purposes.

But we cannot keep on growing and bearing fruit for the kingdom of heaven without remaining deeply rooted in God, and returning to him for regular refreshment.

> . . . When we look at an ancient tree reaching high up to the clouds, we know that its roots, deep in the ground, must be correspondingly powerful. If the roots did not stretch down into the dark depths of the earth, as deep, perhaps, as the tree is high, if the mass and strength of the roots did not parallel the size and weight of the visible part of the tree, they could not nourish the tree or keep it upright – the lightest breeze would blow it down. So it is in man's spiritual life.[5]

As you step forward into the second year of your child's life, resolve to remain rooted in Christ and nourished by him. Jeremiah 17:7–8 says:

> But blessed is the man who trusts in the Lord,
>   whose confidence is in him.

He will be like a tree planted by the water
>that sends out its roots by the stream.
It does not fear when heat comes;
>its leaves are always green.
It has no worries in a year of drought
>and never fails to bear fruit.

Act and pray

Read the parable of the sower in Matthew 13:1–9, 18–23. Buy some seeds as a symbol of new life and, perhaps with the help of your child/children, plant them in your garden, or in a pot indoors. Pray that you and your child/children would be good, fertile soil, ready to receive God's Word. Bring God your dreams and aspirations for the coming year.

If you've got time

1. Matthew 17:20 says, ' . . . if you have faith as small as a mustard seed, you can say to this mountain, "Move from here to there" and it will move. Nothing will be impossible for you.'

   What apparently impossible thing would you like to see God do next year? Ask him for this now.

2. Look up Matthew 7:17–19 and John 15:1–5. How do these verses challenge you? What fruit do you hope to bear this year, and how is God pruning you in preparation?

3. The psalmist often thanks God for past blessings as a way of affirming his faith in God for the next step. Use Psalm 92 to thank God for his blessings this past year, and to entrust yourself and your family to him in the year ahead.

'I have always found it almost impossible to imagine my children beyond their current stage. Childhood is all about immediacy. But you don't keep your baby – their future is like a series of amazing gifts, all still unopened. It's hard to imagine that there could be a better gift than the one you have now, and yet somehow they and we emerge into the ever-transforming present. How can we believe that one day life with the wriggling, giggling babe that occupies our every moment, whose mood we can interpret from a look, will be a fading memory? Life will be full of football kits and ballet lessons, wobbly teeth and sleepovers. We can't hold on to the present. We must let it go, just as we must let our children go into the unknown of their future.'

Joy, mum to Isaac, ten, Caleb, eight, and Moses, one

 Related to this theme:
Month 10, Week 2: Laying foundations for parenting

Profile of a mum

Focus: Looking ahead

Looking back on the past year, it has been amazing to see our tiny baby turn into a toddler, with her own personality. Now I am interacting with a little person! It is incredible knowing that she is part of me, and that everything I do with her is helping to create the person that she is growing up to be.

Some of the highs of the year have been seeing Ella giggling, and also how we have become a family of three. This is a good thing for all of us, although it has changed my relationship with my husband, James, and with friends and family. James and I don't have as much quality time together as before, and at the moment I am often so tired that I find myself being short and snappy with him more than I used to. It's no reflection of how I feel about him – I think it's due to lack of sleep over the past year.

James and I are now trying to put time into actually going out together on our own. We have always felt fine about getting a babysitter so that we can do something at church or help someone out, but we've felt a bit awkward about having a babysitter just so that we can go to the cinema.

My relationship with God has also changed dramatically this year. I need to be in church every Sunday now, because it is one of the few times in my week when I have some space to be with God, as the rest of my life feels so busy. If I miss church for just one week I feel a bit lost, because I haven't had that time with God. I know you can spend time with him whenever and wherever, but for me at the moment Sundays are essential. When Ella was really little, I would just put worship music on and walk around the house with her, but now she wants to play and needs to be watched all the time, so I don't have the same chance to detach myself from her at home.

I realize now that God really carried me at some points during the past year, especially after the first few weeks, when people assumed I was OK and didn't pop round as much, and I had a screaming baby to deal with. At times I felt really lonely. I didn't realize it back then, but now I can see that God carried me.

Motherhood has been all that I expected, and better. I did have some idea of what it would be like from seeing my sister become a mum four years ago. About an hour after I had Ella, I said to my husband, 'I could do this again!' It is amazing how you can love a baby so much. I also feel that God has really developed me as a person through becoming a mum.

Jenny, mum to Ella, twelve months

Your notes

Notes

Month 1

Week 1

1. Matthew 2:7–11 and Luke 2:8–16.

Week 2

2. Michael Wilcock, *The Message of Psalms 73 – 150: Songs for the People of God* (IVP, 2001), pp. 222–223.
3. Hilton C. Oswald, *Psalms 60 – 150: A Commentary* (Augsburg Fortress, 1989), p. 429.
4. Michael Wilcock, *The Message of Psalms 73 – 150: Songs for the People of God* (IVP, 2001), pp. 222–223.
5. Joel B. Green, Scot McKnight and I. Howard Marshall (eds.), *Dictionary of Jesus and the Gospels* (IVP, 1992), p. 604.

Week 3

6. Stormie Omartian, *The Prayer that Changes Everything: The Hidden Power of Praising God* (Harvest House Publishers, 2004), pp. 198–199.

Month 2

Week 1

1. Richard Foster, *Prayer: Finding the Heart's True Home* (Hodder & Stoughton), p. 179.
2. Basil Hume OSB, Cardinal Archbishop of Westminster, *To Be a Pilgrim: A Spiritual Notebook* (St Paul Publications and SPCK, 1984), pp. 203–204.
3. Michael Counsell, *2000 Years of Prayer* (Canterbury Press, 1999), pp. 527–528.

Week 2

4. See Luke 2:22.
5. Basil Hume, *The Mystery of Love* (as quoted in Margaret Long, *The Wedding Present: Riches of Spiritual Wisdom for Life's Journey*, Gracewing, 1999), p. 77.

Week 3

6. 'Take my life and let it be', Frances R. Havergal, 1874.

Month 3

Week 1

1. The books referred to here are *The New Contented Little Baby Book: The Secret to Calm and Confident Parenting*, Gina Ford (Vermilion, 2006) and *The Baby Whisperer*, Tracy Hogg with Melinda Blau (Vermilion, 2001).

2. Chris Ledger and Wendy Bray, *Insight into Perfectionism* (CWR, 2009), p. 33.

Week 2

3. Hannah Ward and Jennifer Wild, *Guard the Chaos: Finding Meaning in Change* (Darton, Longman and Todd, 1995), p. 16.
4. www.apni.org – Association for Postnatal Illness.
5. For information on support during post-natal depression, see the Resources section on page 230.
6. Angela Ashwin, *Patterns Not Padlocks: Finding Christ Among the Chaos* (Eagle, 1993), p. 30.

Month 4

Week 1

1. 'Enjoy', a podcast from the Wide Awake series by Erwin McManus, Mosaic church, www.mosaic.org, 24 November 2008.

Week 2

2. Matthew 16:13–23.

Week 4

3. The *Daily Telegraph*, 19 February 2010, by Rebecca Smith.

Month 5

Week 3

1. Dietrich Bonhoeffer, *Meditations on the Cross*, edited by Manfred Weber, translated by Douglas W. Stott (Westminster John Knox Press, 1998).

2. J. Philip Newell, *Each Day & Each Night: Celtic Prayers from Iona* (Wild Goose Publications/The Iona Community, 1994), p. 27.

Month 6

Week 1
1. Gary Chapman, *Toward a Growing Marriage* (Moody Press, 1996), pp. 162–163.

Week 4
2. Sister Stan, *Gardening the Soul: Soothing Seasonal Thoughts for Jaded Modern Souls* (Pocket Books/TownHouse, 2003).

Month 7

Week 1
1. Donald Miller, *Blue Like Jazz: Nonreligious Thoughts on Christian Spirituality* (Thomas Nelson, 2003).
2. Donald Miller, *A Million Miles in a Thousand Years* (Thomas Nelson, 2009).
3. Ibid., p. 59.
4. Ibid., p. 160.

Week 4
5. D. Guthrie et al. (eds.), *New Bible Commentary* (IVP, 1970), p. 455.
6. As quoted in Sister Stan, *Gardening the Soul* (Pocket Books/TownHouse, 2003).

Month 8

Week 3
1. *Prima Baby*, March 2003.
2. Kenneth E. Bailey, *Jesus Through Middle Eastern Eyes* (SPCK, 2008), pp. 121–122.

Month 10

Week 2
1. Patrick Kavanaugh, *Raising Children to Adore God: Instilling a Lifelong Passion for Worship* (Chosen Books, 2003), p. 119.
2. *The Life of Saint Teresa of Avila by Herself*, translated by J. M. Cohen (Penguin Books, 1957), p. 23.
3. Christina Rossetti (1830–94), as quoted in *The Lion Christian Poetry Collection*, compiled by Mary Batchelor (Lion Publishing, 1995), p. 89.

Week 3
4. John Bimson, *The World of the Old Testament* (Scripture Union, 1988), p. 57.
5. Rachel Barton, *4 a.m. Madonnas: Meditations and Reflections for Mothers and Mothers-to-be* (SPCK, 2007), pp. 72–73.

Month 11

Week 1
1. Ellie Margesson and Sue McGowan, *Just the Two of Us: Help and Strength in the Struggle to Conceive* (IVP, 2010), p. 28.
2. Patrick Kavanaugh, *Raising Children to Adore God: Instilling a Lifelong Passion for Worship* (Chosen Books, 2003), p. 85.

Week 4

3. http://news.bbc.co.uk/1/hi/education/8441207.stm, 5 January 2010.
4. For more on *lectio divina*, go to http://www.lectiodivina.co.uk
5. Angela Ashwin, *The Book of a Thousand Prayers*, quoted in Michael Counsell, *2000 Years of Prayer* (Canterbury Press, 1999), p. 559.

Month 12

Week 1

1. Derek Kidner, *Psalms 73 – 150: A Commentary on Books III, IV and V of the Psalms* (IVP, 1975), pp. 332–333.

Week 2

2. Trends in maternal mortality report: 1990 to 2008, http://www.unicef.org/media/media_56006.html, 2 February 2011.
3. Angela Ashwin, *Patterns Not Padlocks* (Eagle, 1992), p. 103.

Week 4

4. Metropolitan Anthony of Sourozh, *Living Prayer*, quoted in Margaret Long, *The Wedding Present: Riches of Spiritual Wisdom for Life's Journey* (Gracewing, 1999), p. 97.
5. Archimandrite Sophrony, *We Shall See Him As He Is*, quoted in Margaret Long, *The Wedding Present: Riches of Spiritual Wisdom for Life's Journey* (Gracewing, 1999), p. 2.

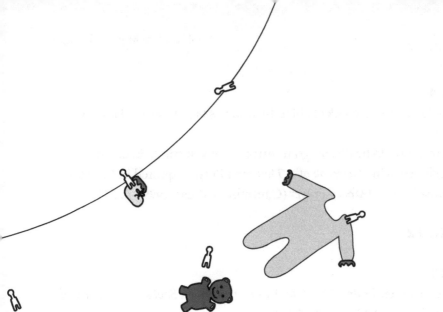

Appendix: Resources

Books

Devotional life

Angela Ashwin, *Patterns Not Padlocks: Finding Christ Among the Chaos* (Eagle, 1993).

Rachel Barton, *4 a.m. Madonnas: Meditations and Reflections for Mothers and Mothers-to-be* (SPCK, 2007).

Catherine Butcher, *A New Mum's Special Gift* (CWR, 2010).

Laura Martin, *The Mother Who Seeks After God: Daily Devotions for Busy Mums* (Christian Focus, 2007).

Alie Stibbe, *Barefoot in the Kitchen: Bible Readings and Reflections for Mothers* (BRF, 2004).

Equipping you spiritually for motherhood

Margaret Hebblethwaite, *Motherhood and God* (Geoffrey Chapman, 1993).

Lindsay Melluish, *New Baby (Bible Readings for Special Times)* (BRF, 2006) – A booklet of daily Bible-reading notes for use during the first month of your baby's life.

Mary Pytches, *77 Bible Studies for 21st Century Mums: 10-minute Pick-me-ups for Mums Under Pressure* (Monarch Books, 2001).

Naomi Starkey, *Good Enough Mother: God at Work in the Challenge of Parenting* (BRF, 2009).

Susan Alexander Yates, *And Then I had Kids: Encouragement for Mothers of Young Children* (Baker, 2002).

Prayer

Michael Counsell, *2000 Years of Prayer* (Canterbury Press, 1999).

Heather Harpham Kopp, *Praying the Bible for your Baby* (Kingsway, 2002).

Stormie Omartian, *The Power of a Praying Parent* (Kingsway, 2006).

Cheryl Sacks and Arlyn Laurence, *Prayer-Saturated Kids: Equipping and Empowering Children in Prayer* (NavPress, 2007).

Practical parenting books

Anne Atkins, *Child Rearing for Fun: Trust Your Instincts and Enjoy Your Children* (Zondervan, 2004).

Ross Campbell, *How to Really Love Your Child* (Authentic Media, 2006).

Joyce Hughes, *Will My Rabbit Go to Heaven? And Other Questions Children Ask* (Lion Hudson, 1988).

Nicky and Sila Lee, *The Parenting Book* (Alpha International, 2009).

Lindsay and Mark Melluish, *Family Time: The Book of the Course* (Kingsway, 2002).

Rob Parsons, *The Sixty-Minute Mother* (Hodder & Stoughton, 2009).

Parenting alone

Diane Louise Jordan, *How to Succeed as a Single Parent* (Hodder & Stoughton, 2003).

Care for the Family, www.careforthefamily.org.uk/spf
Cheer Trust, www.cheertrust.org

Post-natal depression

Hazel Rolston, *Beyond the Edge: One Woman's Journey out of Post-natal Depression and Anxiety* (IVP, 2008).

General interest

Christine Caine, *Can I Have and Do It All, Please?* (Integrity Media Europe, 2010).
Emma Ineson, *Busy Christian Living: Blessing Not Burden* (Continuum International, 2007).
Tricia McCary Rhodes, *Sacred Chaos: Spiritual Disciplines for the Life You Have* (IVP USA, 2008).

Radio stations

Premier Christian Radio, www.premier.org.uk ('Woman to Woman', their show for today's Christian woman, is on air at 10.30 am – 12 pm weekdays).
United Christian Broadcasters, www.ucb.co.uk

Websites/Blogs

www.pray-as-you-go.org
Daily prayer for your MP3 player

www.sacredspace.ie

Ten-minute daily prayers as you sit at your computer
www.mybeyondtheedge.com

Hazel Rolston's blog on post-natal depression
www.desiringgod.org/blog

Charities that support women and/or children

Acacia pre- and post-natal depression support services
www.acacia.org.uk
Action for Children www.actionforchildren.org.uk
Bliss www.bliss.org.uk
Breast Cancer Care www.breastcancercare.org.uk
Care for the Family www.careforthefamily.org.uk
CompassionUK www.compassionuk.org
Refuge www.refuge.org.uk
Save the Children www.savethechildren.org.uk
Stop the Traffik www.stopthetraffik.org
Tearfund www.tearfund.org
UNICEF www.unicef.org.uk
The White Ribbon Alliance for Safe Motherhood
www.whiteribbonalliance.org
Women and Children First UK www.wcf-uk.org
Womankind Worldwide www.womankind.org.uk
Women's Aid www.womensaid.org.uk

DVDs

Rob Bell, Nooma – 'She'

Parenting courses

The Family Time Parenting Children Course – www.family-time.co.uk
The Parenting Course – www.htb.org.uk/parenting

Bibles for under-fives

Nick Butterworth and Mick Inkpen, *Stories Jesus Told* (Candle Books, 2005).
Text by Christina Goodings, illustrations by Annabel Hudson, *Lift-the-Flap Bible Stories* (Lion Hudson, 2008).
Sally Lloyd-Jones, *Tiny Bear's Bible* (Zonderkidz, 2007).
Sarah Toulmin, *Baby Boy Bible* (Lion Hudson, 2006).
Sarah Toulmin, *Baby Girl Bible* (Lion Hudson, 2006).